100 WAYS TO GET PEACE

ASHOK GULLA

Contents

Contents

Contents

Contents

Contents

Preface

Most people like to have some peace of mind in their life. They will be happy to forget their troubles, problems and worries, and enjoy a few moments of inner calmness and freedom from obsessing thoughts. But people wish peace along with all other things which take away peace. It is usual to acquire possessions, feel panic about any failure, sit on judgment on other people, leave no opportunity to criticize other person, hold on to past grievances, and remain always competitive by outwitting other person. People feel pride and respect by holding all that which keep mind busy, stressed and not able to create loving and sympathetic attitude about other people. In addition to these thoughts, people cherish for peace of mind.

Peace is that state of mind which brings harmony within and outside. Of all the things in life, the most important for a human being is to practise peace. Peace is a state of quietness. It is freedom from disturbance, anxiety, agitation or violence. It is harmony, silence, calm, repose and rest. Peace is the very nature of the soul. All the chatting of the mind are dissolved in the soul. There is no thought left in the soul. The presence of God fills heart. This presence through meditation and devotion brings peace. Peace is a divine attribute and need of the soul.

Peace is the happy and natural state of man. Mind remains disturbed due to stress, worries, anger, multiple thoughts and lot of aspirations. It becomes difficult to control unwanted thoughts that take away peace of mind. We cherish for success, prosperity and fame and hope that it will lead towards satisfaction in life, onset to peace and bliss.

We generally blame others for creating an environment of stress within us. The search for peace thus confines to changing others rather than looking within as how to modify own thoughts and behaviour. Peace of mind is an internal matter. It must begin with control on own thoughts and behaviour. It is from peace of mind that a peaceful perception of the world arises.

It will be difficult to relate peace with enjoyment. It indicates desire for enjoyment is uppermost and peace is only secondary to the main desire. People often talk of peace and enjoyment in similar connotation. The real peace comes to a person who gives equanimity to both enjoyment and suffering. How can you be at peace at the moment of suffering when you look for enjoyment? Real peace comes when various distractions of mind are reduced. It has little to do with achievement and success.

Peace of mind is a state of inner calmness and composure, when various thoughts of worries and pain cease and there is less stress and pain. Such moments can be experienced while remaining engaged in some kind of an absorbing or interesting activity. The process of diverting mind from multiple thoughts and worries bring inner peace. This requires searching for moments of peace and to learn about activities that bring peace into daily life.

This book describes various issues we face on a daily basis that creates stress and anxiety, and deliberates on activities, emotions, thoughts and aspirations that need moderation so as to create an environment of peace. As we deliberate on the issues that remain hindrance to attaining peace, it may help in moving a step towards bringing peace and calmness in our life. The topics are not in any particular sequence and not required to read them seriatim. I have gone through various topics available on the internet and acknowledge it in compiling this book.

Ashok Kumar Gulla

CHAPTER ONE

FEELING HURT

It is difficult to remain at peace when impacted by hurt feelings. It is not easy to get rid of hurt feelings as self- ego takes offense when someone deals in the wrong way. People react in a different way when they are treated badly by others. Most of us try to reiterate back immediately showing full anger towards the other person. However, it may not be possible all the time, as the other person may be perceived to be higher in status or elderly in age. The first thing that a person who desires to bring inner peace and calmness is to learn how to deal with hurt feelings.

If a person is not able to offload these hurt feelings, it makes him feel bad. Mind tries to find answers and justifies for becoming hurt. People may think that they should pity themselves when criticized, and that compassion brings a little relief. However, as we pity self and feel hurt, the feeling becomes intensified. An oversensitive person frequently suffers in vain and nobody gets any idea that he has a grievance. So these feelings further hurt a person in self-created isolation. Nothing is accomplished by silently brooding over some alleged offense. It is best to remove such causes of being hurt through ignoring and forgiving the cause that produces such thought. To have a control on the feelings and emotions is at the heart of inner realization, a basic of spiritual training.

It is not correct to presume that everyone will be careful with us. People generally have different perceptions and do not think alike. There are bound to be differences with people. Some people feel offensive and try to disgrace us. Let our thought not magnify the incident. It may be true that other person is at fault to make us feel hurt. It does not mean that person may be wrong, however the manner of interaction may be unpleasant. He may be lacking in politeness. Let us avoid blaming both self and other person, so as to come out of hurt feelings. It is better to leave it at that stage, as a bad interaction, without analysing further as who is to be blamed. Feel pity for his behaviour. Person with whom we are interacting may be selfish and manipulative. All these negative attributes in the other person ought not to entrap us and make us hurt. Part of the responsibility for feeling hurt remains with us. With regular practice, mind learns to not react in an over sensitive manner. This brings lot of quietness in behaviour. As we feel hurt with the behaviour of other person, it is equally important that our actions ought not to make other person feel hurt. We have to be careful to deal with other person with respect, care and sympathy even in the midst of differences with that person.

The best approach to deal with hurt feelings is to bring spiritual awareness. A person who gets influenced with spirituality does feel love, compassion and affection towards others. In such a condition, he does not notice hurt feelings with the intensity which otherwise someone who values self-ego. People with spiritual essence often develop broader perspective to the day to day happening. It is normal with such experiences to think to love and understand other person. Constant practice achieves continuous progress. Every opportunity to interact with others is to rise above negative feelings, to express love and kindness to one who has misbehaved with us. The more we analyse and use our intellect will add to these hurt feelings. It is only by bringing broader perspective in life that helps in dealing with ego and reducing hurt feelings.

CHAPTER TWO

FINDING FAULT

It is common to find fault with others when something is perceived to have gone wrong. The fault could be with surroundings, system, policies, government or people with whom we are dealing. It could be with the way other person talks or the manner in which some task is accomplished. Finding fault do not make things better. The moment we find fault with others, they become defensive. They will provide lot of explanations for justifying their approach. It leads to arguments and counter arguments. In turn, other person may also point fault with us. People get into the habit of putting blame on others without trying to resolve the problem. Finding fault prompts us to avoid taking responsibility. It is cause of stress and takes away peace from our life.

Let us communicate our concerns without finding fault with other person; offer help to improve the way things are accomplished; suggest alternative approach, if any to accomplish a particular task. The manner to accomplish a particular task varies from individual to individual. We may observe that our subordinate, colleague or spouse are not able to perform some role effectively in a manner would have liked it. The capacity of a person to accomplish any work depends on his/ her overall knowledge and interest in a particular task. Complaining and finding fault will either create inferiority complex or resentment in other person.

The words spoken ought to be modified to achieve our purpose; it needs not to be directed to humiliate or find fault with other person. All these things, if adopted in life works wonders for imparting happiness and regaining self-esteem of other person. Words spoken could either make somebody hurt or happy. Hence, we have to be careful in choosing our words even when confronted with adverse situation. This will make atmosphere charged with happiness and we will get happy vibes from other person. It in turn makes our inner condition peaceful.

Sometimes, people get into habit of criticizing or fault finding others without any genuine reason. It may be just for pampering personal ego. Much of the trouble in this world comes due to personal ego. Someone wealthy or on high position in job, feels important and treats others not with equal respect. It thus starts with fault finding. We have to understand that other person in return can also find fault with us, as we may have several deficiencies that other person find painful. It will continue as a blame game, and atmosphere becomes non-cooperative. To create harmony with other people, we have to ignore little irritants, and to move ahead in life with peace and happiness. It needs strong moral character for the person well placed to treat people below him with love and respect. This is what is expected of a person who is in tune with spirituality. He will feel less impacted by his higher status and much in tune with others; love will flow from him.

Married couples spend considerable time together and often get into the habit of finding fault with each other. They develop differences on various issues and resort to anger, argument and fault finding. It needs reality check periodically by internal introspection to satisfy that mine behaviour do not bring any ill feeling to other person. All these things are known to us but need is to put it in our practice and make it part of personality refinement. Let us avoid finding fault with others for own sake, to bring a peaceful discourse in our life.

CHAPTER THREE

RESPONSIBILITY

People who are responsible meet the challenge and feel less panicky when faced with a task. Being responsible makes them to remain calm unmindful of pain and aches that come with the day to day problems. They are proactive in dealing with problems and plan well to meet any challenges. These people do not need to rush at the last minute. Responsible people are well organized, more focused and efficient to overcome the problems with less of pain. Due to this behaviour, they are found to be at peace.

A person who acts in a responsible manner does not blame family for his personal problem. This makes the atmosphere at home more congenial even in the face of difficult situation. Similarly, person who acts with responsibility works hard to meet challenges at the professional level. These people avoid putting blame on others and do not like to pass buck on someone else. The feeling of being responsible comes when a person is able to connect with others, and does feel to work for the common good. He feels comfortable without expecting similar contribution from other person. At office, he prefers to take lead and discharge his role, despite the difficulties encountered. This generates respect and other person responds positively, without shrinking his role. At home, he tries to discharge major activities, thereby reducing the pressure on other family members.

A person acts in a responsible manner, if he is man of reliability. Such people feel that solution to the problems have to be sought by them, and nobody else will help to sort the problem without their full involvement. They do not like to put burden on others. These people develop more immune system and live longer and remain happy in a productive manner. They feel encouraged from past successes to meet any difficult challenges. These attributes are desirable to create an environment of peace and happiness.

These people plan properly and take proactive steps to overcome problem. They are able to deal with various tasks without rushing at the last moment. People who do not own responsibility expect others to work and remain dependent entirely on somebody else to sort their problem. They try to postpone discharging their responsibility till the last resulting in chaos and panic.

They are not able to perform well and blame others.

On the contrary, responsible people eat well, exercise frequently, treat others with respect, interact well in social settings, have good friends, and become exemplary role models for others to imitate. They quickly recover from sad situations, move on, and become productive once again. These individuals learn from the mistakes made by others, avoid trial and error approach to solve the problem. They do take calculated risks and make mistakes, but they learn to not constantly repeat previous errors.

When a person acts in a responsible manner, he realizes that peace and happiness may remain unattained, if looking for an ideal situation with no problems and conflicts. He realizes inevitability of problems and tries to derive satisfaction by resolving them with commitment. This attitude of owning responsibility goes long in creating an environment of peace and happiness.

CHAPTER FOUR

PRAYER

We generally remain stressed as mind always thinks about competing, outwitting and fighting with others. Prayer is a powerful means to overcome such feelings and cleans inner self from this dirt and make it abode of peace, love and happiness. During prayer, think of love, truth, sincerity and hope. All these are divine attributes. All of us during prayer visualize that God is taking care of us and all other creations.

More often, our attention during prayer again goes to materiality while the true meaning of prayer is to explore on the immaterial aspects of life. God, please give me a good house, a good looking spouse and a good job. God, please curse the person who has troubled me. God, please give me wealth and richness. The dialogue goes in similar fashion so as to gain in material possessions. It again puts pressure on mind to think of these as the ultimate means to derive peace and happiness. Instead of releasing mind from these worries, we try to bring importance of these in our life.

During prayer, let us seek help from God to love others. Pray to God to make us sincere in our dealings. Feel gratitude for God and other people who have helped us. Pray for the welfare of others. Pray for bringing compassion, truthfulness and simplicity in our attitude. By doing so, we are attaching importance to these virtues. Every time we pray for something, it creates a scintillating impact and energizes us to act in that manner. People who offer sincere prayer are often observed to be loving, grateful and compassionate.

How can you communicate and pray to someone whom you have never seen, known or talked. Prayer cannot be effective unless we develop certain capabilities to feel HIS presence. This reminds us of inner consciousness (soul) which is a spark of energy flowing from divine. Believe that the essence of God is lying within you. Feel HIS presence all the time with you. Prayer is a way to remember God. The advantage of prayer is that you talk to someone who is perceived to be Powerful, Righteous, Creator and Knowledgeable. This is how everyone perceives God. With this faith, you try to pray for HIS blessings. Thus prayer removes ego as you perceive someone bigger than you, it helps to modify behaviour as you may not pray for doing something wrong. Prayer brings strength when you face trouble as

HE is seen to take you out of these miseries.

Prayer is refreshing for mind as also it revitalises soul. Mind feels troubled with the negative emotions as these are contrary to our inner consciousness. We may like to hate or feel angry on someone while our inner self always yearns for love, sympathy and compassion. As mind and inner self are pulling in different directions, it is a source of tension and stress. During prayer, we work internally to create loving feeling for all the people by realizing the essence of God. If prayer is sincere, it brings patience and tolerance to overcome difficulties through the medium of prayer and devotion.

A sincere prayer connects you with other people. You realize that every other person is aiming at the same thing, love for God. The similarity of purpose brings love, familiarity and cooperation. The prayer diverts attention from problems and helps in creating peace.

CHAPTER FIVE

COMPARISON

The main reason for losing peace is to compare with people who are perceived to be better in some respect than us. To compare with colleagues and if they have progressed well, it makes us in some respect feel unhappy. It is common to feel that other people are lucky, be zealous about their success, and blame on our luck and circumstances. The comparison is mostly with people who are higher in ladder of success compared to us. Despite these comparison, there is no clue about whether such material possessions, success or any other things possessed by them which is lacking in us has really made them feel better.

The people perceived to be better in material possessions than us may not be happy. Look to total possessions, someone is better placed in one aspect, but may have to struggle for something else. You may be low in material possessions but blessed with good health. Hence comparison is mostly illusionary in nature. We are not able to judge whether all those things which are not possessed by us will really make us happy. Let us compare self with people who are perceived to be lower in material possessions and status than us, it should make us feel grateful. Comparison ought to make us feel kind and sympathetic towards such people.

Comparing with someone and feeling bad for things not possessed is main reason for losing peace of mind. It troubles us lot and drains our energy. We do not enjoy whatever have already possessed. Look to life in totality; make a list of successes and failures; it becomes evident that each success has its price. A successful person in one field may not necessarily be successful in other areas of life. A good paying executive may be facing problem in his personal life. A wealthy person may not be maintaining good health. The comparison that makes us depressed is often based on false assumptions and limited knowledge of other person. A poor man may be happy and contented; he may be getting respect and love from his wife, maintains good health, and his children may be possessing good qualities that brings satisfaction to the parents.

Why we compare with others? It is to satisfy our ego and to see our self to be superior. This is the reason that people like to compare with others who are better in some respect. They aspire for same level of possessions that someone better in status has already acquired. They do not look to peace and calmness but something to make them feel superior. It is natural to lose peace of mind and happiness when efforts are directed towards something else. Comparing with others creates negative emotions; it often leads to inferiority complex. We try to find and search for various reasons as why we have been left out. This search makes us to find fault with the system, with the people with whom we are working or to put fault on self or on our family. Ultimately all this analysis and thinking leads to worries and depression.

Being egoistic may be constructive to drive a person to perform better and be more focused. However, at the emotional level, these qualities create problem in being too conscious of how others deal and perceive you, possessive of various material comforts and expectations level remain high. People who have control on Ego are simple and sincere with less of inner turmoil. They prefer not to glorify their achievements and not to hide their failures or ignorance. They do not feel need to always compare with others. This keeps them at peace with their possessions.

CHAPTER SIX

INDECISIVENESS

"There is no more miserable human being than one in whom nothing is habitual but indecision, and for whom the lighting of every cigar, the drinking of every cup, the time of rising and going to bed every day, and the beginning of every bit of work, are subjects of express volitional deliberation" [William James Varieties of Religious Experience].

A mind which is continuously thinking and not able to decide remains disturbed. The major cause to remain turbulent is indecisiveness. When people have varied choices, decision making often becomes difficult. We think there are always 'good choices' and 'bad choices' in life. It often becomes difficult to find out which is good and bad choice, as every choice has its own advantages and disadvantages. It is premature to label any action as completely good or bad. Our attitude largely determines what we make out of particular choice.

Every one of us suffers sometime due to indecisiveness. If it becomes habit, it can affect us adversely in terms of self-confidence and peace. Life provides various opportunity, we have to encash these opportunity at the right time. These opportunity may not repeat again. People who are successful act fast, avail of various possibility for business and professional growth, learn from failures and move ahead. Indecisive people generally think lot about negative factors and turn towards others for assurance to deal with these issues, and in the process delay taking any decision.

You may be able to decide a right course of action, but the decision delayed in the hope of selecting a better choice takes away its benefit. The ideal approach is to make best use of our choices. We often repent about certain bad decision made in past. However, while taking that decision, we may not be aware of all the pros and cons of various choices available which unfolded later. It is not proper to repent about past decisions as it depends on so many factors on which we do not have full control. We can turn a bad decision to our advantage by proper planning and efficient manner of implementation.

It is not only our indecisiveness, but indecisiveness of people around us that also affects calmness and peace of mind. At offices, if the boss is indecisive, it creates confusion and focus on particular task is lost. Indecisiveness leads to delays and loss of opportunity. Many times we lose good opportunity due to indeciveness.

When not confident about making a decision in life, it is tempting to just avoid them altogether. Instead we keep on thinking and building stress. Perhaps we become indecisive after a bad event, or having lived in fear of doing the wrong thing. Regardless of the root of our indecisiveness, we feel frustrated and powerless.

As an indecisive person, one of the first thing to do is stop over-analysing. This tendency comes from the fact that we do not trust our self. We continuously think about how others will perceive it. Thus the need is to tune emotions more accurately and develop finely perfected insights. Let us understand that there is no absolute good or bad decision as it depends on circumstances which are not completely under our control. Stop blaming self for taking decisions that might have gone wrong and move ahead with poise and confidence that will restore peace of mind.

CHAPTER SEVEN

FEELING ANGRY

We often think that other person has not treated us well, tried to harm, and is taking undue advantage. This creates anger when something happens contrary to our expectation. While these scenarios are often not rational, but still we accumulate anger. We tend to shower our anger to subordinates, spouse and family members. This has become habit with many people to fix responsibility on others. When we sense some challenge; our mind generates fear and anger. At many times we feel angry over a trivial issue. Even when the issue at stake is small, but mind tries to justify the anger by creating various scenarios. The anger is real and powerful, even though reasons for being angry are not always real.

People accumulate negative emotions over a period of time and it bursts in anger. The cause of the anger may not be immediate reaction, but something else. It takes time for other person to understand exact cause of anger. It leads to confusion and ill feeling in a relation. It often happens at work place when superiors insult and put lot of demands on our time or criticize about performance. This anger and feeling of insult gets accumulated within and it needs to be vented out. We come back home with mixed feeling of anger and humiliation hidden and wish to be left alone. At that moment, we feel irritated if family member talk about anything and vent our anger and frustration on our spouse and other family members.

People fail to appreciate the real cause of anger, and remain unhappy in a relation. In a married relation, even though the anger is directed towards you, but the problem may be somewhere outside. These days life has become complicated; professionals who earn well are expected to achieve tough business targets putting tremendous pressure on them; it makes them panicky and angry. People have forgotten to relax.

Getting angry does not lead to somewhere and the situation may even become worse. If we are too much emotional, it makes us overreact on various issues. We often remain angry on trivial issues. Anger does much harm to us than to the person against whom it is vented. People try to justify their anger by amplifying the issue and entire energy goes towards arguing with other person. Many problems in life get resolved smoothly when we remain calm and attend with confidence without feeling angry.

Anger is a by-product of fear. The fear of losing superiority, self-respect, ego, authority and possessions is at the back of many angry outbursts. People need to look within to find out what things make them angry. They might have failed in meeting their own aspirations. This also makes so many people sceptical about various things in life. They try to find fault with everything happening around them. They feel irritated and angry. Anger increases blood pressure and makes us to feel uncomfortable. It is imperative to understand the need for control of anger. While outside situations may not be within our control, we have to work within to control tendencies of anger.

Pause for a few moment before bursting anger and introspect whether the situation can be handled differently. Ignoring various irritants while dealing with other person, is one of method to control anger. Let us introspect every time we feel angry and find the reason behind it, and ways to avoid it for own benefit so as to be at peace.

DIVINE JUSTICE

People often feel that their efforts are not adequately rewarded. There are number of instances when someone who is not sincere, hardworking and intelligent is well placed in life. In comparison, person who works hard may be struggling. It is difficult to comprehend this dilemma. Then people who appear to be genuine are often seen to suffer. Often, legal system and Government are not able to provide fair justice. The question arises is there any super power that takes care of all these infirmities. Is there something like divine justice and how to believe in it?

We observe that in this world the good and evil deeds of men are not subject to any fair accounting in terms of justice. Criminals and oppressors encroach on men's lives and their freedom and many times also enjoy opulence and luxury until the end of their lives. It is logical to think that honesty, sincerity and hardworking ought to be rewarded and manipulative practices to be punished. However, this does not always happen. There is something called *law of Karma* as prophesied in Hindu Religious Philosophy which means that every action, whether good or bad has its impact in the broad dimension of our existence. There is the element of surprise in natural justice.

People generally conceptualize about events and deeds in a narrow span of time and space. Divine frame of reference is bigger and much large both in terms of time and space. This is the biggest mystery of our existence, and time and again it baffles us and creates lot of apprehensions and misunderstandings. We presume that results of our actions and deeds ought to be pronounced immediately. Someone who has done wrong ought to be punished immediately within one year, two year or may be in immediate future. Natural justice time span is longer as life from the perspective of divine does not end with this life, but continues with lives thereafter and so many lives earlier. It is therefore logical to think that rewards and punishments need not to for this life but are carried out to lives earlier and thereafter. As per Hindu religious philosophy, our actions, good or bad, get attached with the casual body (soul) as *samaskaras* (impressions), from one life to another, and have to bear fruits of these actions.

Science is not able to comprehend this as it is beyond

its present capabilities. However, we often talk of luck and psychologists talk about genetic condition for being happy and depressed. They have not been able to explain fully why a person due to its genetic conditions will be better placed than others under similar conditions. I think the answer to both lies in broader time span of divine justice. What is luck? It is a favourable environment in which a person is placed due to his good deeds earlier. The law of action (Karma in Hindi) which is considered a divine law based on Hindu Mythology applies equally to all. According to it, all actions have a reaction and when a good deed is done, it results in good reaction. Our knowledge of divinity being so poor, it becomes difficult to comprehend everything which is divine. Losing faith in divinity and its justice do not lead to anywhere. So many things are happening around us which will be difficult to explain. We tend to become selfish, manipulative and greedy when we lose this bigger picture of large span of our real existence. People are able to resolve many problems of life by bringing this perception in view. Divine justice is not only a matter of faith but a reality. Believing in Divine justice brings peace both in adverse and favourable situations.

CHAPTER NINE

TACTFUL

The present world gives lot of importance for being tactful. Professionals are asked to be tactful in discharging their duties. By 'Tactful', people often mean 'Not revealing full truth', 'thinking about self- interest' and 'outwitting others'. Rarely, people use tact in a positive manner.

In the name of being tactful, we try to suppress full truth and make untrue look like real. People feel pride in revealing only what is considered beneficial or less damaging. These tactics are used often to devoid other person from a rightful claim. Since all the acts of tact are performed within the framework of legal system, it gets legitimacy and are not challenged. They feel whatever is done within the rule of law is acceptable. However, there is bigger purpose in life which is not completely laid down by societies and legal system.

Some people are by nature tactful. Even where no tact

is required, they still prefer to suppress information and make other person feel uneasy. People often use tact to show their importance and make small things look complicated. There need not to be any tactfulness in adopting good values in life, like love, honesty, contentment and simplicity. It is therefore desirable to shun tactics when it is not in tandem with our inner consciousness.

Being straight forward is in tune with our moral ethics. You may be in an advantageous position to deal with the other person. Your demanding nature, aggressive ways and oppressive language may be your way of being tactful in getting things done. You are within your right to create such a stressful atmosphere for the other person. However, is all that not stretching too far? Think for a while, are you supportive, considerate and compassionate in your behaviour?

More often than necessary, tact is used in the negative sense, to gain advantage over others. Tact gives you enough scope to twist the real truth. Tact is an act of mind. It involves lot of thinking as how to be tactful. Often, we observe conflict within as whether to listen to the mind or abide by the feelings of heart. As long as tactics is used to deprive others of comforts, respect, love and compassion and we participate in such tactful activities, it is damaging for our inner growth, personal values and morality.

It depends on each individual, whether tact is used to deal with the other person in more compassionate manner or to create difficulties. Tact can be a virtue of good character that suggests a person is deeply considerate of the feelings and beliefs of others. To be tactful requires a sense of understanding of what is appropriate and proper when dealing with others.

Being tactful can also be manipulative act. It depends on how you use it. Nobody may be able to challenge you. It then is left to you and your inner consciousness. Remember, inner self will always remind us that these tactics are not in tune with its liking. People try to ignore these cries from inner self and suppress them. These may be beneficial in one way but they do not create any value that you may cherish in the long run. Look to the broader picture of life and use tactics in the positive manner. By doing so, when tact is adopted to help others, it will create a positive environment of peace around us.

CHAPTER TEN

PERSONAL VALUES

Personal Values are not dictated by law, profession or society. They are principles that define us as an individual. These are inner feeling that directs us to respond to a particular situation. How we interact and understand other person is largely outcome of our personal values. People who reinforce some of the good values in life based on truthfulness, sincerity and integrity are observed to be warm, affectionate and sympathetic towards others. The inner feelings and beliefs affect and influence decision making and relationship with others.

The capacity to judge others is influenced by what we think as the important aspect of life. Is it success, co-existence, tolerance, truthfulness, fair play or manipulative practices? A person who values success as the single most important aspect of life will often try to outwit others, at times through coercive means. His dealings with others will be based on how much he can be successful in the relationship. Success and achievement alone are not sufficient to bring satisfaction in life. This is because the perception of success and achievement may not be in tandem with inner need.

For someone truthfulness and tolerance being important aspect of beliefs searches these in his actions. The most important aspect of personal values is that they filter information and help to judge what is right and wrong. This is the reason for people to react differently in a similar situation. When people try to hold good values, truthfulness and tolerance comes naturally. This reassures their inner consciousness that they are moving on a right path.

Without fully being aware, we stand for something which appeals to us as convenient. This becomes personal value for us. It is easy to say that success, wealth, friendship, aggressiveness, ego are good for you. However, when these are taken to extremes and misused, they can be damaging.

Personal values are difficult to assess, and not easy to value. You cannot with certainly say that certain beliefs and values are good or bad. This is the reason that people often justify their personal values as right, and hold on to it irrespective of damaging them as a person. How much people benefit from love, respect and gratitude towards others is difficult to evaluate. Nevertheless, they are useful and help us to lead a satisfying life. Value of these personal attitudes from material perspective is difficult to assess. This is the main reason that we are not able to appreciate the values of many things happening around us that are perceived to be useful. Personal Values may not have any immediate benefit but these create environment for leading a satisfying life.

Personal values are for attaining inner peace. Values help to bring the broader aspect of life into focus, and not to over emphasize on negative emotions. Personal Values are essentially outcome of inner dialogue that directs to make better choice when faced with complex situations. The importance of personal values lies in its adherence and making these as part of our way of life. We believe that certain values are good for us; these are true and need to hold on these for all times irrespective of their benefit or otherwise. These values guide us; they become a purpose of life. Adopting good values based on love, trust and gratitude is a way towards attaining peace and calmness.

CHAPTER ELEVEN

EASY LIFE

When we talk of living an easier life, it often means doing very little, laziness, less aspirations and taking no responsibility. Living an easy life is perceived negatively in the present world when people are expected to be busy, stressed out and competitive to enable them to move ahead in life. Present materialistic pursuits have made life complex. People do not know how to relax even for a few minutes.

Living an easy life has a different meaning that can be perceived by one who brings broader purpose in life. It means eternal bliss and peace achieved through practicing contentment, gratitude, control on impulsive mind and unconditional love towards other people. As we bring all these attributes in our life, we notice life to be easy irrespective of difficulties and troubles that usually make a person stressed and worried. Unfortunately, most people overlook these intangible values in life as they feel it cannot bring any immediate benefit.

Life is easy if we live a balanced life taking care of physical, emotional and inner need. While wealth and other material comforts satisfy need of body; self-esteem, recognition and maintaining good relations with friends and relatives help to achieve emotional need. Besides, we have to feel connected with God and other people through love and positive feelings to satisfy the need of soul. People who avoid to improve such inner capacity remain turbulent, selfish and egoistic. People detest easy life and expect it to be competitive to remain ahead of others. One can be competitive and achieve his goal, and simultaneous remain internally connected to real-self by adopting attitude to live easy life.

The most important factor that can make life easy is to not worry about rewards of our action. A person who does not believe in the divine power keeps on thinking about result of his actions and blames destiny. If immediate rewards are not received makes a person tense and stressful. He feels to have been deceived and cheated. He blames others and become cynic. However, a different thinking is held by the person who develops faith in divine power. He does not get bogged down with rewards as his faith in natural justice makes him to believe that divine will take care of him. He prefers to wait for the results of his actions

Life is complex in nature and it needs special efforts to enjoy an easy life. Our ego and superiority complex makes us to desire for more material possessions. Being complex in your attitude, material possession and lifestyle is a status symbol. People do not like to be left behind and avoid adopting simplistic approach. It is however for our own good to think whether all these complexities are worth accumulating. The simple lifestyle will be possible if we feel absorbed for some time with our inner self.

We have too many aspirations in life. It is difficult to achieve all that in shortest possible time. If we think of material possessions, it may take time to accumulate but often we do not enjoy fully all these comforts due to short life span and lack of capability to enjoy these comforts. We spend entire life hoping for material comforts but it lacks in providing long lasting happiness. A balanced life where wealth, material comforts along with building loving relationship and focus on inner calmness have to be pursued all together for making journey of life easy.

CHAPTER TWELVE

SILENCE

Silence is one of the many attributes of the Divine including peace and love. As thinking is an attribute of the mind, feeling an attribute of the emotions, silence is an attribute of the Divine. In the modern world, silence has practically ceased to exist. It is very difficult to go anywhere where there is no possibility of being disturbed by the sound. Living in the midst of all this noise have a bad effect on remaining at peace.

We live our lives in the midst of mechanical noise and it produces an undercurrent of agitation inside us, produced by the noise. This noise is one of the reason for mind to be stressful. This lack of quietness has also meant that people are no longer used to silence. Along with inactivity, silence has become something which most people are determined to avoid. Remaining silent means remaining idle and it is considered wastage of time and efforts. People have become so used to remain active that they feel uneasy when left with nothing to occupy their attention even for a few moments.

Along with external noise, our mind is constantly disturbed by the chattering of our ego. This chattering fills mind from the moment we wake up in the morning till the moment we go to sleep at night, an endless stream of daydreams, memories, deliberations and worries. We have no control over these noises, which even continues as dreams when we fall asleep. This 'inner noise' has as many bad effects as the mechanical noise outside us. It actually creates problems in our lives, when we grudge over tiny inconveniences or uncertainties which seem to become important just because we are giving so much attention to them. We continue to discuss about all possible future plans and these occupy mind and make it stressful.

Silence provides opportunity to spend time with inner self. When not interact with other person, our attention goes towards our self. We find time to remain in remembrance of Ultimate. This time is also utilized for organizing and planning. We do not react instantaneously, but respond after considering all pros and cons. Silence prepares to deal with the issue in mature manner. We have to practise silence to avoid putting burden on mind. When we remain silent, we feel the presence of pure consciousness inside us. Silence is a refreshing activity. People often argue with others to prove their knowledge, expertise and understanding. This attitude puts us always in competition with other person, and it makes us feel exhausted. Different people have different perception and faith. The understanding on various issues differs. We feel turbulent when other people do not agree to what we believe. It is for our own good to be more discreet in deciding when and how much to talk. We may offer our views without making others to feel bad.

The silence has its own advantages. We are not in conflict with others while remaining in silence. We allow other people to judge and understand us. Our actions and deeds talk for us. Maturity of a person will be reflected when he talks limited and purposeful. We need not to defend our actions all the time. Remaining silent when not required to talk will enable us to remain absorbed in good thought about our blessings; it activates us to do good deeds or be in remembrance with the Creator. Our inner calmness will be enhanced if we try to adopt silence and give other people due respect to listen to them.

CHAPTER THIRTEEN

INTROSPECTON

Introspection is observing oneself with an unbiased perception involving examining own thoughts, feelings and sensations to gain insight. Our fast paced lives hardly give us enough time to stop, think and make decisions. Decisions taken in haste only make us repent later. People who are important to us in our life will have their own opinions about what we should do. It is not a bad idea to ask for the opinions of people who matter to us. While we may take their feedback, introspect about it but finally we do what we think is best for us. Hence, self-introspect is to re-examine at regular intervals about what we stand for, and efficacy of it to take us happily and persistently through the course of life. The situations may change rapidly, and accordingly course of life need to be adapted to meet these challenges. This calls for introspection at every stage of life. Let us sit at the end of day for a few moments, and find out what troubles most and are these worth holding.

Some things in life will unfold exactly as we desire. But, most things may not really happen according to our whims and fancies. Sometimes, events that occur may not be as per our expectations. When we introspect, we can see the big picture, which will teach us to be at peace with the situation. When we look at things from a larger perspective, we will understand that certain things are beyond our control and it is better to go with the flow. This will not only make our lives easier, but will also bring peace and happiness.

Introspection is a wonderful trait and not many people have the time or desire for it. Our busy lives and preoccupied minds rarely provide us the time to introspect. In order to introspect, one must first quieten the mind and look inwards. Life provides lot of diversity and full of aspirations. People work hard to accumulate wealth as a major priority in life. At the same time, to enjoy life and develop fruitful relationship is other need. Lot of temptation is for self-gratification. This often becomes main focus of some people. Other need may be to think of developing love, tolerance, sacrifice and enlightenment for self- improvement and long term inner peace.

People often lose track in life due to varied aspirations some of them are mutually contradictory. On pursuing all these aspirations create distraction in life. Life has to adopt a direction to remain focused in pursuing a particular goal. Hence, it requires introspection at regular intervals to find whether life is going on right track.

We cannot be good hearted person if carry lot of ego and superiority complex. To think of love and sacrifice is not possible if we are selfish in nature. We may not generate peace of mind if busy all the time in amassing wealth. It is therefore desirable to prioritize life and focus on core values. People may believe that whatever the consequences, they will like to remain sincere in dealings with others, helpful to others, hardworking, courageous and ambitious to reach their goal. Think what you like to aspire in life. Introspect to decide where energy and efforts need to be spent. What are the things that make you unhappy and are all these worth bothering? What we have to do to turn out to be better in our own perception? What we need to do to develop inner calmness? The fear of losing our prestige, wealth and possessions haunts us. Let us examine whether we need to shed some of these fears and move ahead in life in peace.

CHAPTER FOURTEEN

CONTENTMENT

Peace in life depends on level of contentment. We might have expected life to be ideal in so many respects, but despite best efforts, things might not move the way we would have liked. Some people move ahead satisfied with whatever comes in life, remain contented and try to ignore things not achieved. It does not serve any purpose to feel dejected and make life more miserable. We will be doing injustice to own self, if continue to feel dejected and dissatisfied with what we did not possess. We lose the enjoyment of things that we actually hold, by remaining in a state of dissatisfaction. On the contrary, when we are content, our happy times are happier and sadness is less sad.

Most of our attention is drawn in meeting outward desires and these do not subsidize. Each desire when fulfilled rise to fresh set of desires. While we may make all the efforts to acquire and amass wealth, and derive comforts by making use of this wealth, but we may restrict to limited desires. This will be possible by divert our mind from desires towards realizing higher purpose of life. Life is short, it will be misfortune to spend it only in meeting desires. The state of contentment comes when we draw our attention for some time from external world and remain absorb to realize our inner self. This reduces outward distraction and fills us with peace.

Avoid comparison with people who are perceived to be better than us in material possessions. Fill life with more intangible values like love, sacrifice and honesty as it will help us and other people around in bringing happiness.

Feel gratitude for so many things which God has provided that ought to make us contented. Every one of us will be blessed with so many good things, but we often ignore them and crib about things not possessed. Look to what we have which most others are deprived. A loving family, normal health and a stable income; most of us have all of these. Are not these sufficient reason to be contented, but we look for big house, costly vehicles and fancy articles; wish list is never ending.

Let us Love others; make other people happy; and share their worries and anxieties. These activities meet our inner needs and make us feel happy and contented with life. We feel capable to achieve what is aspired and it makes us contented with life. People who engage in pursuing some higher goal in life remain busy and excited leaving no time to feel dissatisfied with life.

Contentment in life is realized by proper balance in life. Everything in life; job, family, relations, rest, enjoyment, wealth, all contribute to overall life satisfaction. We cannot feel satisfied by ignoring anyone at the cost of other aspects of life. Living a balanced life brings contentment. Enjoy your possessions; you will be having number of these; look around and feel satisfied. Derive satisfaction from day to day happenings. Do not postpone it for big events. Big events will rarely come; learn to derive contentment from life as it folds before you.

Think of broader purpose of life that emphasizes on looking to inner –self (soul) for making us to concentrate on intangible like love for others and remembrance of God. This leads to contentment with our possessions and achievements. Expectation will be at the minimum and we will try to give more in the relation than receive it back.

LIVE IN HARMONY

Living in harmony requires taking care of yourself and others with equanimity. It is the need of divine and ultimate truth to not discriminate in any way. Compassion is a feeling to be useful to others, and mitigate their sufferings. This feeling comes naturally – it simply works through you on your way to spirituality.

People are generally selfish in nature. They wish to take care of own self-interest even at times at the cost of others. However, as people develop inner capabilities to love, respect and feel compassionate towards others, it makes them to take care of others as much as they look after self-interest. This single act makes people to be straight forward, truthful, and considerate towards others. A step towards taking care of other, demands sacrificing own needs for the benefit of other people.

The present day problems and troubles, whether they are economic, political, religious or social, but the root cause is not to emphasize on living in harmony. Nations and society are competitive and do not feel need to emphasize on living in harmony. Legal system in most countries falls short to reinforce harmony among citizens. We try to live a self- centered life taking care of material possessions, wealth and professional achievements, but ignore the common welfare of other people around us. All attention goes to self-growth and glory. This makes us to be in competition with others; we treat other people our competitors who need to be won over by any sort of tactics.

Living in Harmony talks of equanimity despite outward differences. The deeper we delve into spirituality, the better we appreciate that all human beings from the divine perspective are equal. The external differences in knowledge, wealth, colour and religion are too peripheral and need not to predominate our thinking. Spiritual perspective talks of deep inner connectedness with other people. Living in harmony will come naturally after a person understands the importance of love, compassion, forgiveness, empathy and humility. These are spiritual virtues which come on the journey towards understanding real purpose in life. Differences will look too feeble with others when the attention is directed towards real self.

Living in harmony is feasible only when we are sensitive

to other person's suffering. Compassion means to understand and show kindness to others when they fail or make mistakes, rather than judging them harshly. Finally, it means that we realize that suffering and failure is part of the human existence and has to learn to live with others despite these imperfections. Understanding others' plight and living in harmony is a natural response to our love for other person.

Nothing can create profound impact on dealings with others than acts of compassion and empathy. It may be a small gesture that puts other person's interest ahead of self-interest. With acts of compassion, it is to bring the inner connection with other people and God, as no other way will be equally effective. This is the reason that people who wish to move ahead in their spiritual pursuit look for living in harmony. Look to your inner self; it shows extreme level of happiness and peace when we develop capacity to be in harmony with other person. To take care of others and remain at peace naturally arise to a person who lives in harmony with others.

CHAPTER SIXTEEN

HATE

Hate is not only damaging for other person, but it also spoils own self. A person who has the tendency to hate other person often feels stressful. He does not live in peace. Look to family relation these days, despite lot of material comforts, people are not happy. The reason is emotion of Hate has taken place of Love. True love is missing in most relations with family members, colleagues and friends. At slightest pretext, we get enough provocation to hate someone. The reason is that mind has been trained to think in this manner. It needs lot of efforts to clean our self from this feeling. Hate is the cause of all the trouble, wickedness and other sins committed by human beings.

Take away HATE from all human beings to make world a place worth living. All of us ought to pray for this from God. How much stressful we feel in life because of the hate accumulated against others. Our perspective of life takes extremely negative view due to this emotion.

We deem other person incapable, unworthy and a threat to us. At times, we accumulate hate against someone, without any valid reason, but swayed by emotions. Think for a moment how do you feel without any hate feelings against others. This leads to self-discovery. True purpose of life will be realized if we unseat hate lying within us.

Mind is at the centre of all evil. We have spoiled mind and it now behaves in an erratic manner. We do not like someone merely because mind has created a wrong picture of that person. It does not stop at that. The next step is to combat with other person and to take revenge. This is the work of mind to create a feeling of hate against other person; in most cases without understanding fully other person. Having decided to hate other person, it directs to take revenge against other person in whatever possible manner. This is the starting point for crime, greed and corruption. Suppose, our mind does not allow us to think badly about other person; it will be difficult to think of harming someone. All other acts of crime will subsidize significantly. Hence, origin of all the crime is feeling of hate.

The biggest culprit is the mind. If we control the mind, we are deemed to have won the love and respect of the people. This is not a wishful thinking but true. Look to great saints. They have control on their mind; it makes them to think about good of the other people. Hate does not come to them. They are able to influence large section of the society through their love.

Hate works contrary to the need of inner- self (soul). We have to realize that our true self comprises both body consciousness and inner consciousness. God expects us to keep inner consciousness in focus while dealing with others. Inner-consciousness is nothing but a feeling of Love. Unfortunately, we ignore this inner need and adopt selfish attitude towards life. This brings hate in our dealings with others; onset of all troubles, miseries and cruelty. Hate is the work of devil lying within us as love is the divine energy flowing from God. Unless we destroy devil in the form of hate lying within us, we will not be able to realize true self.

The greatest paradox which all of us face is to know the true purpose of life. The best way to solve this is to shun hate and bring love in dealings with other people. This will bring more and more awareness about our true self and inner bliss. Let God help all human beings to shun hate.

CHAPTER SEVENTEEN

FORGIVENESS

Forgiveness helps us to let go off the anger and look to the positive side of the relation. It is very stressful to be continuously at war with our self. By thinking about what harm others have done to us will not in any way do much better. We may think that other person has given a raw deal, but it may not make much difference in the behaviour of that person. Finally, it is self-defeating to complain about others as it further damages the relationship. When things get tough, and we are troubled by the relations, forgiveness helps us to acquire enough strength to calm down our negative thoughts.

How many times we feel hurt, angry and insulted with the other person's behaviour. We have been taught to not take it lightly and fight it back. Our mind prepares us to fight for justice. It creates different scenarios as how the other person has dealt with us, and tries to justify our stand of becoming hurt and insulted. More often, our intellect tries to magnify the situation so as to justify that something grave has happened, and we need to reiterate back with full venom and force. Often, the real cause of feeling angry or insult might be trivial, but we continue to suffer, as very few people think of alternate way of dealing with the situation. Is not it worth to forgive and forget. Forgiveness and forgetting others mis-behaviour towards us is for own benefit to remain in peace and develop positive attitude. Imagine how much time we spent in criticizing others, blaming someone and feeling hurt. We lose the capacity to forgive and forget unpleasant incidents.

There are going to be differences and disagreements with so many people on so many issues. The key is to understand the unavoidability of disagreement and to move on with love. This needs attitude of forgiveness. The ability to remain in peace when you do not get what you want from others is forgiveness. The decision to remain in pain and anger or to forgive it is ours. If we hang on with the situation, it may not do any good to us. If other person does not do any work as per our wish; we feel annoyed and mentally disturbed. However, if a person has inflicted great damage to us, or assaulted physically, forgiveness may not come easily. We may not be able to forgive a criminal. In such a situation it is better to pray for own calmness and forget the incident while taking appropriate recourse to deal with the person.

As we develop spiritual essence, our inner condition looks for eternal peace. Our mind tries to look inward. It avoids feeling bad towards others. People who adopt path of spirituality do not easily notice any fault in other person. They remain ignorant about anything bad spoken against them or any harm met on them. Even if they notice any harm inflicted on them; it is of little consequence. The mind does not remain bogged with these incidents, it looks for oneness through love and compassion.

If we are not in a position to forgive other people including our close relations and family members for all the pain inflicted to us, it may be difficult to carry on with life filled with love. We have to empty our vessel inside from bad feelings through process of forgiveness and then to fill it with love. The other option is to fight within for the pain and anger accumulated over a period of time. People who look to God to protect them in case of difficulties find great solace and tend to forget and forgive others.

CHAPTER EIGHTEEN

MISTAKES

When anything goes wrong, it is natural tendency to not admit mistake and put blame on other people, system and circumstances. The first reaction is that we are not at fault and it is someone else who is responsible. This makes us to fabricate lot of lies to hide truth. The mistake may be too trivial but we feel it below dignity to admit and rectify it. Especially, people who are well placed in life never like someone to point mistake on them. They prefer to have yes man around them so that their shortcomings are not reflected and known to others. Superiority complex and arrogance always comes in our way to remove small mistakes which often become source of irritation for others.

If not able to perform any task well, we try to hide mistake and feel tense and burn out. As we hide our shortcomings, it brings more stress. We are not able to live up to own expectations. When people admit mistakes, they are relieved; it unburden mind from hiding truth. It is possible that other person appreciates your truthfulness and pardons these mistakes. However, people are often found to not admit mistake. They drag on till the last to justify their actions. This is the result of lot of anger and negative emotions. In our family relation, we put blame on spouse; while at office, it is common to blame juniors for not discharging their role effectively.

Let us learn to admit mistakes for own good. It will do lot to make us lovable to others. This simple act when performed by so many people will take lot of anger and hate from the society. Let people not always boost about their achievements. Pause and admit your mistakes. It needs inner strength to admit mistake.

Mistakes can be of different nature. It can be in understanding and doing a particular task; it could be in wrongly treating other person. At the particular moment, you may be busy, stressed out or angry on certain issue. This may lead to certain mistakes. As you pause and come out of the stress situation, you realize having committed some minor mistake either in performing a particular job or treating other person. You will make someone feel happy if you admit mistake in dealing with him. You will gain respect from other person.

Admitting mistake leads to inner purification. It is good for inner calmness. Holding on to mistakes creates negative emotions, it further goes to curse the person who has highlighted such mistake. It leads to spoil of relations. A small act of admitting mistake unburdens from all such emotional baggage and helps in restoring peace. It provides scope for doing things without repeating such mistakes in future. Let ego not come in our way to make things complicated. Admitting mistakes makes a person humble in the presence of other person. The dealings will be based on trust and truthfulness. It is possible that other person will also realize that he has to admit his mistakes to you. There is always scope to improve.

It is not sufficient to admit your own mistakes. How you behave when someone does something wrong is also equally important. If people admit their mistake in front of us, we ought to be generous in not making a big issue of it. As we learn to pardon others for small mistakes committed, it brings truthfulness and transparency in dealings with others. People will not fear to hide something from you. The environment will thus become cordial and peaceful.

CHAPTER NINETEEN

CHANGES

Change in life is a normal process. People become sad and depressed with the routine changes in their lifestyle, relations, job profile and environment around them. Change demands certain adjustment. It creates uncertainty for some time. We fear about adapting to the change. When people are not prepared for any change in life, it creates more stress and turmoil. They are not able to plan properly about change. How many of us have felt depressed because of change in relation, job, income and place of stay. While change brings uncertainty, it also offers new opportunity. It makes a person to understand other person better.

If someone suggests change in our lifestyle and attitude, we become defensive. We expect all others to change but not own self. Life is a dynamic process and nothing remains static for a long time. We have to learn to change with the circumstances. If something is not useful for us, let us not hang on with it, and keep on justifying it.

There are certain issues in life that are cause of much worry. We are not able to do anything as we expect other person to change but not our own self. Changes in life are unavoidable. Let us not resist each and every change in life; it makes life stressful as we are not prepared to face these changes. We may initially face difficulty to adapt to these changes, but eventually these are for our benefit, it provides new opportunity, and makes us to learn from these changes. People who desist changes, are not able to live life peacefully; they are filled with negative emotions and fail to live life as it unfolds. It is better to prepare self in advance about changes that are going to unfold, and plan accordingly.

If health spoils, it needs change in eating habit and lifestyle. There is no point in cribbing with the changes required in life. Similarly, adapting to the requirement of job requires to change and improve professional skills. People often desist these changes and lose opportunity to grow in life. We are not able to understand the changes required in relationship when we grow from child to adolescent to a young couple and then a responsible parent. Every time it requires us to take care of the new challenges in a relation. As young couple we are too close and intimate. As life progresses, relations redevelop and it is better to appreciate and adjust with these changes. People unfortunately curse these changes and often remain unprepared to face the life as it unfolds before them. We lose a great opportunity to cherish the present moment of life by cribbing about the changes in life, most of which are beyond our control.

Changes in life provide opportunity to reinvent self. Find the changes worth picking and carrying through the life. When something goes wrong, people feel shattered and try to find excuses and put blame on others. This is the time to find what it makes to remain strong and to have inner resolve to change for the better. We think of only those changes that bring comforts. People shun changes that are uncomfortable. This is the reason for our aversion to changes in life. Let us understand that life is not always comfortable, painful, successful or unsuccessful. With every pain there is a comfort and with every success there is a failure. These are relative in nature. A person who is used to comforts of life is troubled with slightest pain. Adapting to the changes in life derives inner strength and calmness to face the life in a satisfying manner. People lose great opportunity in life by cribbing always about the changes in life.

KNOWLEDGE

It is normal tendency to pose knowledgeable and discard other's view point as trivial and insignificant. This habit has become common with so many people who try to behave as professionals and experts. You think to be knowledgeable compared to other person. This is the basic presumption which most of us carry while interacting with others. People often argue and try to prove their knowledge by outwitting other person.

Knowledge have many dimensions and everyone has own view point on various issues. This makes people to remain unreceptive to the views and feelings of others. They try to hang on to their knowledge without interacting fully with the other person. We observe how many people feel irritated, angry or stressed out if their view point is challenged during a discussion.

A knowledgeable person is one who understands and helps and not competes with other person. Let knowledge be not used to make other person feel low and inferior. However, this is often the way we use our knowledge. At office, seniors try to show their knowledge to dominate juniors. In home, show off of knowledge builds barriers between married couples rather than creating close bondage. Knowledge is vast and no one can be fully conversant. We have to provide enough opportunity to other person to explain his point of view.

Knowledge ought to bring humility and not arrogance. It has to be acceptable to people at large and not conflicting in nature. More and more people ought to accept and respect your knowledge. It ought to make you wise and tolerant to the divergent view point. We find truly knowledgeable people depict all such qualities. Such people will never boost of their knowledge. Let knowledge not create barriers with other people. If a person becomes egoistic about his knowledge, it does much damage compared to its real benefits.

Knowledge ought to add wisdom. This is the true knowledge. Let people not boost of their knowledge, it is a small drop in the ocean of wisdom. Many people who are not knowledgeable in the literally sense have abundant wisdom. Great saints and reformists, most of them are not fully knowledgeable, but still they influence people due to their broad vision, wisdom and commitment to certain cause. Is your knowledge making you wise? We observe through experience, that understanding and knowledge keep refining as we dwell more deeply. Our knowledge and understanding are likely to undergo change, it ought not to make us behave arrogantly. Being knowledgeable is to help society and spread it for the benefit of others. This is way to connect with others, by offering support in areas where we are expert. It is a step towards developing positive feelings of love and satisfaction.

Wisdom is a deep understanding of people, things, events or situations, enabling to choose or act to regularly produce the ideal results with a minimum of time and energy. Wisdom is the ability to optimally apply perceptions and knowledge to produce the desired results. It is understanding of what true or right is coupled with optimum judgment as to action. It often requires control of one's emotional reactions so that one's reason and knowledge prevail to determine one's actions. The need is to acquire wisdom. To boost about knowledge indicates low in wisdom. One can remain in peace by not boosting about knowledge and to be receptive to the divergent views. It will keep us to remain calm during interaction with others.

CHAPTER TWENTY-ONE

SUFFERING

The problem with most of us is that we try to avoid suffering at any cost, and think it should not come to us. Hence, when faced with suffering, we are least prepared; it makes us depressed. These sufferings cannot be completely eliminated from our lives, as when we try to enjoy life, it could create moments of suffering. Our health, wealth, profession and relations while providing comforts in life can be source of suffering. That does not mean that we ought to shun our wealth, profession and relations. We do not have any control on our suffering. What cannot be avoided, let us face it. Let us not presume that things will turn in our favour every time.

We pray for comforts, and remain worried about any possible suffering. The more we remain worried about any suffering will make us incapable to face it when it falls on us. Life is combination of both enjoyment and suffering. For some people, a small discomfort appears to be suffering and they feel depressed. Any suffering also provides strength to face it. It makes us strong, humble and connected to other people. Let us analyse the suffering, to find whether it is due to our fault and what can be done to learn and perform better in future. Suffering can be sometimes due to negative feelings, without any tangible loss. Let us not be bogged down with suffering, it comes in one or the other way, but think of how to face it. The difference between a happy and depressed person is that both face suffering to a varying degree, but happy person faces it with challenge while the other person fears about it.

If we are not able to avoid suffering in the course of life, it is better to take it in our stride and do everything to pass it with less pain. We are not the only person who faces these troubles. As long as we do not get anxious and irritated, then our strength of mind will enable us to bear even the hardest of sufferings easily; they will be trivial and easy to face. But while we are dominated by anxiety, even the tiniest problem becomes extremely difficult to cope with, because we are burdened with anxiety.

Once we are convinced that we have to live in this life with both joy and suffering; we will not avoid it but learn to develop a sense of joy and resilience even during suffering. This unfolds bigger purpose of life;

spiritual essence that derives meaning to our suffering to bring inter-connectedness with others, reform in our attitudes and realization of real self. Yet whenever suffering strikes, unless we have some kind of spiritual practice to bear with it, one which matches the capacity of our mind, it is extremely difficult to remain at peace and calm. It is extremely difficult to use suffering as the path towards spirituality and self-awakening when it has already struck, and is staring in front of our face. It is crucial to become familiar with the specific practices and strong spiritual conviction, to fall on when misfortune and difficulties befall us.

Suffering can become a help for our spiritual practice, but that alone is not enough. It is not only our suffering; we have to count on blessings. The sum total is to feel contented with both suffering and blessing. We may find how we have been able to overcome past sufferings, and how we have felt happiness on overcoming such sufferings. This may make it clear that both suffering and happiness are not completely separate. Let us resolve that now onwards, I need not to worry about suffering as it will move me to more permanent happiness and bliss.

PRESENT MOMENT

The present moment is the most valuable in our life. Past and future are equally important for successful life, but past had happened in the past. We cannot go there because time always continues to go on. Future will be there waiting for us. We can make most of our future if only we make most of today. So let us utilize our time at present in the most effective manner.

What is the point in regretting about past, worrying about the past mistakes and difficulties that came in our past. Then people plan about future and dream about it without doing anything concrete in present. People find comfort in remaining either in past or in future. They only think about things they have to do in future, but do not give much time to find the ways to do that work in time. It is always better and healthy to learn lesson from the mistake we had made in the past and forget those obstacles. There will be ups and downs in every one's life. Happiness will depend on our present moment.

People often live in past or in future. A considerable time is spent dealing with past grievances or glorifying past events. We recall these past events and bring in our deliberation with others. Alternatively, we think lot about future and remain worried about future challenges. In the process, people spoil their present moment. The most important time is present. This is the time to rejoice, enjoy, feel relaxed and be of use to others. Unfortunately, people are bogged with either past or future events, leaving little time for the present.

Mind does not stop thinking various things at any point of time. It remains distracted. Living with past grievances impacts working to full capacity in the present. Mind does not get free to concentrate on the present event. The need is to forgive others for any trouble inflicted in past, so as to free our mind from these bad emotions. Learn to live in the present and feel the importance of the person with whom we are in contact.

Mind remains stressed by bringing so many issues at a time. We are not able to enjoy the present moment, but are busy thinking either about past or future. Mind keeps on wandering and these distractions affect our peace. We fail to appreciate the goodness, malice, sadness or generosity of the person with whom we come in contact. If we devote time and efforts to present activity, it will help in shaping for better future. Whatever we are doing at the present moment is most important job for us.

We fail to enjoy the present moment by diverting mind elsewhere. Remaining focus on present will make us to enjoy life better. We will be able to devote our self to the problems more effectively and make other people feel important by offering undivided attention. People who are effective and productive found to be focussing in present moment unmindful of difficult past or uncertain future. There are ample examples of men who despite troublesome past have focussed their attention and achieved their footprint in this world.

The essence of the life remains in present moment. The activities we carry during present moment will carry us forward. The enjoyment we get in remaining absorbed in present moment is enormous compared to remembering past events. Practise of love, gratitude, understanding and empathy unmindful of past will bring inner joy and happiness.

CHAPTER TWENTY-THREE

REAL-SELF

Knowing own self is to understand aspirations of physical, emotional and spiritual aspects of entire self, and how best to realise these requirements. Understanding all these facets of our existence leads to self-discovery. This brings focus on overall purpose of life and goes beyond meeting bodily necessity of food and shelter. It has to look for the aspirations of inner –self (soul) as we understand our real-self. The focus shifts from momentarily pleasures to long lasting peace, happiness and contentment. We acquire knowledge, develop talent and skill on various subjects to be capable to earn and live comfortably. Despite this, we remain ignorant about our spiritual needs. Our spiritual essence remains hidden and we often try to ignore it. This is the reason for present unhappiness and disturbances.

The basic mistake that all of us commit is to treat self as a body consciousness, and ignore the real self (soul) within it. Look to the needs of soul by feeling its essence. Realize that our self is not body but it comprises of inner essence that is soul. There is substantial indirect evidence about our- being soul and soul being immortal moving from one body to another body. Certain instances have been found where people remember their past births.

Most of our attention is drawn in meeting outward desires and these do not subsidize. Each desire when met gives rise to fresh set of desires. We remain too much busy with meeting needs of body thereby loosing essence of real self. Meditation helps to go deep and perceive real- self. The need is to remain connected with soul by looking within and drawing attention away from external distractions.

The need of real-self i.e. Soul is to remain in love with other fellows despite external differences. When we realize the truth that there is close connection with other people, it will make us to remain in loving feelings with others; it gives us the glimpse of inner essence. We realize eternal bliss filled with love all around for humanity and thereby to God. Negative emotions will reduce.

Spiritual part of our existence expects us to remain connected with our creator, same as child feels happy to be with the mother. If our condition is contrary to what is expected of our inner self; it makes us feel depressed and unhappy. People who generate hate, anger, ego, lust and selfish tendency to satisfy their physical need have emotional set up contrary to need of soul. They feel momentarily happy by external stimulus but lack inner calmness. They are ignorant of real self.

Knowing your self is to be aware of oneness with others; ignoring own ego and superiority complex; thinking of common welfare of others; generating unconditional loving feelings for others, and remain in ignorance of self while fulfilling your worldly needs. If we see all others as a reflection of own self; think everyone filled with same essence coming from one source; feel essence of God within; and realize that every moment other person is with us as our companion, guide and friend. It will remove most of our fears, pain and suffering; bring us into a strange sort of ecstasy: eternal bliss. This condition once pursued makes us to realize and know self and bring long lasting peace. We feel less of turmoil due to happenings around us.

CHAPTER TWENTY-FOUR

LONG LIFE

It is a general perception of so many people that they will not die immediately and hence try to postpone activities that could bring them long lasting peace. People remain busy in activities that help them to earn livelihood. Meeting our daily requirement are essential, but along with this main function, we ought to find what our role beyond it is. The broader role emphasizes on improvement in our attitude and perception of future, able to help others. What is the key driving force that ought to bring satisfaction to our life? Presuming life is going to end in near future, what are the immediate things we need to do? These questions appear to be too hypothetical, but still they create curiosity to move ahead in life with purpose.

The need of body will never subside. Along with this need, it is better to resolve issues that could become hindrance for bringing overall satisfaction in life. Resolve various disputes which trouble you. Bring financial stability by focusing on contentment. Lastly, devote time to connect with your real self. Create tender feelings. The keenness to search for inner peace ought to be pursued along with other activities, and may not be postponed for future. People often believe that they will have ample time at old age to think about broader purpose of life. Old age often gets worse, leaves little time for thinking about self-realization, if we do not prepare well in advance for it.

Life can end abruptly and we lose a big chance to understand real essence of life. Everyone hope to live a full life, and keep on postponing crucial tasks for future. Rarely do we realize that life can end any moment of time. Most of us postpone tackling problems for future, be it personal or professional issues. The real purpose of life is to live it with love, inner peace and contentment. This can come to a person who sees death as a near possibility.

People engage in routine things and keep on postponing real issues for future. It is presumed that future will provide sufficient time to engage in activities that can help in developing honesty, truthfulness, faithfulness and compassion. Any refinement in behaviour and personal values has to start now otherwise it will be never. We realize at the far end of life having wasted life in preliminary and too mundane issues without finding real peace. Everyone knows that life is going to end at any moment, we prefer not to discuss it, it is considered bad omen. Presuming life to continue for a long period does lot of harm, both while living in this life and life hereafter. We are least prepared to complete tasks that remain unfinished, like mending relationship with close relations or settling financial issues. We also do not prepare for our journey beyond death that is assisted by intangible values. Intangible values are essentially borne out of oneness with others through love and compassion. We feel no urgency to adopt these qualities, and remain busy in self- interest.

Realizing that we may not get a long life to live will bring to focus activities that are for common good. The focus will shift from material comforts to generating love, compassion and generosity towards others. This attitude will reduce the ego and mind will learn to remain calm and not in conflict with others. The fact that life is going to be curtailed abruptly will bring long lasting serenity and calmness. We will not crib for so many things and our old age can go with satisfaction. We will have less of regrets during journey of life.

PATIENCE

Patience is the state of being that occurs between experience and reaction. Whether you are trying to be enduring with yourself, others, or life, it seems to always involve the experience of dealing with delays or obstacles. By cultivating a practice of patience, we are able to let go of things outside our control and live with less stress, anxiety and frustration.

When we look at what it means to have patience, we are talking about dealing with own thoughts and emotions. As a spiritual being, there is an unbounded, limitless presence within that is constantly seeking expression. Hence, it requires patience to unravel the broad picture of life. As a time-bound, physical being, we have limitations for experiencing this inner knowledge. We think, act, and experience, and this is the simplicity of life. Problems arise when it does not seem to produce immediate results.

When others let us down or irritate, be patient with them. Gently express love and stillness. Whatever issues we may have with another person are likely to be temporary and will undoubtedly change, it ought not to push away from own plan. What disturbs us now about this person may change and in the next moment we may feel some positive emotion. Regardless of what other people do or think, we have a choice in how to allow it to affect us. Mind may jump to negative notions and reactions, body may even register a response, but we are the source of it all, and can tap it into peace.

When we want things to happen instant, our attention and energy goes to the frustration we feel about waiting. We feel frustrated to wait in a crowd, traffic jam or to meet someone. The waiting is not the problem. It is how we deal with it, how we see it. Practicing patience shifts our attention away from the frustration to inner self. Utilize moments of wait, which may be unavoidable, in the remembrance of inner-self. Spend these moments in recalling enjoyable memories or meditate on inner self, when you are required to wait in a traffic jam or waiting for seeking appointment. Plan in advance to take care of these eventualities, and not to rush for every activity at the last moment. Acting with patience is a way of telling life that you are in charge. You are in no hurry, there is no distress—only peace and confidence in our reality.

It is true that someone very intelligent, hardworking and committed fails to achieve the success that was reasonably justified. On the contrary, people adopting manipulative practices do get benefited from the system. This dichotomy often troubles us. We lose faith in divine justice and think how such things are allowed to happen.

It is better to understand that good action does not get unnoticed. Life does not completely end with death. We are in so many lives before this life and may be so many after this life. It is a continuous process. Any rewards and sufferings of previous life percolate to this life and life hereafter. We are ignorant of who we were earlier, as God wish us to concentrate and do a good job in this life without burdening us with previous memories of earlier lives. However, this does not mean that they have been removed from our consciousness, they are part of inner consciousness (soul), but we are not able to know it. It is normal for all of us to expect rewards or favourable results of good work done. We have to have patience to wait, may be not only for this life but life afterwards to gain from good deeds.

CHAPTER TWENTY-SIX

LISTENING

Listening is not something that just happens like hearing, it is an active process in which a conscious decision is made to listen to and understand the messages of the speaker. Listeners should remain neutral and non-judgmental, this means trying not to take sides or form opinions, especially early in the conversation. Active listening is also about patience - pauses and short periods of silence should be accepted. Listeners should not be tempted to jump in with questions or comments every time. Active listening involves giving the other person time to explore their thoughts and feelings, they should, therefore, be given adequate time for that.

The manner we listen to others is important to gain love and respect for other person. After having established eye contact, it is important to relax. Distractions like phone, books, papers and other things should be put aside as this behaviour will disrupt the process of listening and will give a message to the speaker that you are not interested. If what the other person says alarms you, but do not start on judgment, as it compromise effective listening skills. Let us not jump to conclusions. We should give due respect to the speaker even if we disagree on some of the issues. If the speaker has baffled, we need not to make a big issue of it, and give time to speaker to express his thoughts and emotions. Let us not react immediately but take time to think and then respond. At times, we realize later that we could have reacted differently. Also, let us feel the emotions of the speaker so that to get connected with him or her. Effective listening can avoid anger and bring calmness and peace while dealing with others.

Apart from Listening to others, we may also listen to our inner voice to guide through this life. People are often indecisive and confused between listening to the logical aspect of the human mind or the inner voice of the spiritual self. The brain is centre of planning, analysis, coordination and looks to a particular situation from the perspective of gain and loss. Our inner self sees the bigger picture and is not calculative. Now, people face these situations on a daily basis as whether to abide by what mind dictates or listen to the inner voice from the heart. More often people look to the overall benefit in dealing with others. They naturally listen to mind which provides various scenarios of how best we ought to deal with others to maximize our benefits. Mind teaches us tact, aggressiveness and sophistication to outwit others. In the process, inner voice has been subdued.

Developing intuition is an important step in listening to the inner self. It requires shifting the focus from the chatty mind and external distractions to noticing subtle emotions and sensations in the body. The next step is to ask the inner self for guidance on important topics such as developing future goals, dealing with other people, aspirations and creating satisfaction. When a person is taking action in alignment with their inner self and higher purpose, he feels good.

Listening to inner voice is like communicating to own self. We have to realize that inner self has a connection with Ultimate. Give sufficient time to be with this self away from external worldly distractions. It reminds time and again that this fight is not worth the benefit it derives. It talks about love, compassion and humility as a great force to connect with others. As we realize that every other person is like own self, it brings more rationality and humility in approach. It helps us to deal with external world not as a fighter but one who likes all others.

CHAPTER TWENTY-SEVEN

BALANCE IN LIFE

Life has got many dimensions, and it calls for maintaining balance to meet various aspirations. People put lot of efforts on one aspect and ignore other dimensions of life. People may think wealth is most important thing to be pursued and put lot of efforts to accumulate it. Similarly, for someone excellence in profession is the ultimate goal of life. Similarly, for others remaining ahead of others in chosen field may be the ultimate goal in life. If people are not successful in their chosen area, they feel disturbed. We do not have anything else to look for satisfaction. Let us understand that wealth, health, profession, family, society, love, inner development and being spiritual all have a definite role in shaping life and creating satisfaction. Look to not one but many aspects of life in its entirety and not as a disjoint pieces in your search for gaining peace and satisfaction.

Creating balance is not about doing all the activities

and getting exhausted. It is all about prioritizing, to decide what is important and evaluating how much time and energy you should invest in things that matter to you. Is it really necessary to socialize too much at the cost of your health and family relation? Do you need to gather too much information which may not be of much use and feel exhausted? Can you avoid spending money on luxurious items so that to remain financially comfortable and maintain stability in life. Assessing priorities regularly help to stay focused, effectively manage time, and to prevent burnout are means to maintain balance in life.

The elements in life that require the most balancing can be divided into two categories: internal and external. Often, people focus on one more than the other. For example, you may find that you focus on external things, like work, relationships, and activities, and that you pay very little attention to what is going on inside your heart and mind. On the other hand, you may find that you spend so much time being self-reflective that you sometimes miss out on the experience of living. Maintaining balance in life has to create both external excellence and inner calmness.

People feel that external growth does not go together with inner development. Adopting spirituality means to so many of us about leaving worldly responsibilities and pleasures. They find it difficult to comprehend how to bring all these in the fabric of life. Spirituality means inner purification which is as important as external growth. Living a balanced life means to take care of needs of both body and soul.

Realizing about Inner consciousness helps in searching for broader purpose of life beyond our bodily needs and emotional satisfaction. As we dwell more on this issue and bring our Inner Consciousness to focus in our daily routine and thoughts, it modifies our attitude and dealing with others. Our inner-consciousness craves for oneness with others and God. We do not feel need to come in conflict with others. It makes us to love and tolerate others. We do not take life as a competition to outwit others; but to live in love and harmony. We thus appreciate all aspects of life be it profession, wealth, family and relation and bring balance to all these aspirations only after realizing broader purpose associated with our true consciousness, A narrow view of life means ignoring inner consciousness and getting impacted with bodily pain and pleasures. A balanced life that takes care of both body and soul is a way to generate peace.

CHAPTER TWENTY-EIGHT

GRATITUDE

Gratitude is the feeling of being blessed and of course, grateful. It is the expression of what for am thankful. It includes family, friends, good health and all the gifts in my life. Gratitude makes every day sacred, it is the key to living with an open heart. From the moment we wake up until going to sleep, life presents one opportunity after another to be grateful. This daily practice of gratitude will focus us on present activity. Our life will be enriched when it is seen through the eyes of gratitude.

Gratitude highlights good things happening in our life that reduces the negative impact of adverse situation. Gratitude is one of the most powerful tools for creating joy, healing, contentment, spiritual growth and lasting relationships. Each moment of our lives, we can choose our attitude and where to focus our attention. When people consciously choose to be grateful, even in times of adversity, ability to see the good in life is strengthened. If we focus on everything that has blessed life and made us feel good, we are going to get more of that. The practice of gratitude is life empowering. It can change state of consciousness. To be thankful can shift or pivot the emotions of fear, frustration, depression, or sadness to a lighter feeling.

Feeling gratitude is a way to remain in peace. The moment of gratitude for good things happening in life makes people feel better, and improves their self-esteem. Express gratitude to God for providing us various comforts of life; it brings satisfaction and sense of welfare. Expressing gratitude helps us to cope with the difficulties in life. It is a positive act to express gratitude to others for all the good things done to us; this way we are able to feel connected with others and maintain social bonding. People who cultivate attitude of gratitude are found to be happier and filled with positive thinking. Gratitude reminds us of good things in our life, it automatically diverts our mid from negative emotions and troubles. It strengthens our resolve to work for more such things to be grateful.

Gratitude is one of the most effective means to remain on the right path based on morality and spirituality. It can be easily cultivated requiring daily practice and least sacrifice. It is a very powerful form of mindfulness practice, particularly for people who are prone to depression, self-defeating feelings, and those who always look to the dark side of a situation. Practicing mind filled of gratitude consistently leads to a direct experience of being connected to life and the realization that there is a larger context in which our personal story is unfolding.

When reminded of bad moments in life like troubles in relation, not moving ahead in career, difficulties in dealing with other people; it makes feel bad, lose energy, feel nervous, lose words to express, lack of sleep and disturbance. This negative stuff does lot of havoc to inner calmness.

The practice of gratitude is not a denial of life's difficulties. We live in troubling times and no doubt we experience many challenges, uncertainties, and disappointments in our own life. Still, there are so many people who love, help and support us. Without them, it will be difficult to live at peace and happily. We need to be grateful to all and not curse self. Gratitude is useful because it turns the mind in such a way that it enables to live into life with peace.

ATTITUDE

An attitude is how we view a situation. It involves both a thought and emotions. Whatever may be the situation, each person has certain thoughts about it, and also responds based on their emotions. Hence, it is not only thinking that guides us to react to a situation or deal with a particular person; it also involves emotional response. People may have same knowledge about a particular problem, but their emotional response may differ, and thus they react in a different manner. It may be easier to change the thinking of a person by providing all the data and information; it is not easier to change the emotional response.

Attitude determines to a large extent whether we remain at peace and calm in a particular situation or not. Life is full of good and bad things. People who chose to be sad overlook many good things, get perturbed by the bad things in life and feel depressed. This accelerates many aging processes and the onset of deterioration in health that make people sadder and depressed. We come across number of people who have nothing to feel cheerful, but their attitude drives them to feel happy.

If emotional condition is good, we feel interested to deal with a difficult situation with less of pain and anxiety. It is bad emotions that most of us need to change. When we feel sad, angry, anxious, or frustrated, we do not like it. We want this feeling to quickly go away. So we start trying to change these emotions. But, it is not easy to change emotions, people often justify their emotions and expect others to change, so that to feel better.

To change our emotions, we have to start with our thought process and behaviour over which have more control. Engaging in positive thought process and looking to behaviour in a particular situation will gradually modify emotional feelings. The thoughts, behaviour and emotions are interrelated. To change attitude requires that we think positive and adopt good behaviour.

Developing positive attitudes can contribute to leading a satisfying and peaceful life. It can be developed in our belief that sincerity, hard work and courage will yield good result. People with positive attitude believe that difficulties will not remain for ever. They think that natural justice will help people who adopt a right course in their life. This belief keeps them moving with faith on good virtues of life. People, who believe in right action based on sincerity and integrity, direct their responses to the problems accordingly. Positive attitude helps people to interact with less of conflict and inter-personal relation issues. People with negative attitude feel uncomfortable to work with others, as they crib at the problems. They do not contribute significantly to the well-being of others because they remain bogged down with problems. A person with negative attitude find it difficult to trust someone.

To stay with positive thoughts, the need is to identify negative thoughts that distract and make us feel bad. It could be work related issues, problems at home, dealings with other people or something related to financial position. Try to reduce its impact by attempting to sort out the problem, ignoring its impact or reducing our expectation level. If nothing works, then let us accept the problem and divert our attention from it. There are number of positive happenings in everyone's life. Let us look to these and move ahead.

CHAPTER THIRTY

IMPULSIVE MIND

The impulsive mind is an indication that our emotions need to be directed in a controlled manner. People behave in an impulsive manner when they expect that everything ought to move in a way they deem it right. They have limited capacity to tolerate others and generally adopt knee jerk reaction to various issues. People, who are more tolerant towards others, are found to be calm in nature.

Mind remains filled with thoughts and never finishes thinking and continues to remain busy. People keep on thinking about so many things due to various emotions like ego, fears, desires and expectations. The mind tries to seek answers to satisfy various emotional outbursts. If someone has not agreed to our view point, our emotional response may lead to anger, hate, dissociation, inferiority complex, defensive attitude etc.

Impulsive mind is also a reflection of lack of confidence

in our own self. If a person fails to generate answers to the problems encountered, it makes him impulsive as he tries to look for solutions from somewhere else. The capacity to face problems is greatly affected as we lose patience and look for quick solution.

Thinking and carrying all the bad feelings about others keeps us engaged. In the process, we lose peace and calmness. Mind needs to be given rest by ignoring the past baggage of bad thoughts. These thoughts go on multiplying depending on our fears, expectations, anger, hate and other emotional feelings. It reduces sleep and affects health.

To ensure that mind remains calm and in happy disposition, understand the circumstances that affect and trouble us. People feel trouble and pain, when someone tries to harm and has destructive tendencies. It demands doing all that is necessary to protect ourselves. However, most of the times, people get adversely affected by having different view point and disagreement with others which hurt their ego. When family member does not agree with us; we feel perturbed and lose our inner calmness. Let us realize that each one has his own way of dealing with a situation and understanding on various issues. We need not to get perturbed and our mind not to act in impulsive manner, if someone does not agree to our view point. This realization ought to come on us due to constant control on our thought process to bring humility and empathy towards others.

The external environment will not always shape as per our expectation. When affected by outside circumstances, by losing inner calmness; we let other people and circumstances to dictate our peace and calmness. People who reduce the impact of outside happenings, and resolve to not get disturbed and lose their peace of mind, will gradually increase tendency to look and deal with others as their own. It is equally important to pause and listen to other person so as to understand him better, before our impulsive mind takes offensive of other person. Once we realize closeness with other person, we feel that the trouble and insult met has been given by the one belonging to us. This feeling of oneness is important to reduce the impact of disturbances and troubles in the mind. It can be derived by focus on the need of soul to be in love with other human beings. Meditation helps controlling thought process and focusing on inner self that bring calmness to impulsive mind.

CHAPTER THIRTY-ONE

CONCENTRATION

The people who have capability to concentrate are more disciplined. They are able to prioritize various functions and do not feel stressful. They do not waste time in idle pursuits, but are more focused in their approach to life. To make life more disciplined, it helps in devoting quality time with other person that come in contact. We will be able to generate a feeling of joy and happiness, provided able to concentrate on particular job at a time. The purpose of life is to make a positive impact with as many people as we remain in contact. This is possible when we find sufficient time to interact with others, without diverting too much.

People often remain busy in thoughts either of past or future. The most important for concentration is to focus on our present. The important person at any moment is the person in contact at the present moment. The most important work is the work at the present instance. Let us not distract mind but concentrate on the person with whom we are in the present. Thus we can attend with care, understand other persons' concerns better and make him/her feel happy. We inculcate responsibility towards others, only if able to concentrate and attend to that person.

People when not able to concentrate, do not utilize time effectively; feel burdened with work; return home tired, and remain engrossed in the worries of office. If mind is not able to focus on any particular job, it results in efforts getting wasted. Demanding job and pressing deadlines need us to concentrate, and to focus on the job. However, we often remain distracted, tense and overburdened.

People need to develop various techniques to remain fresh to be able to concentrate fully on particular task. It could be through exercise, listening to music or sitting quietly alone in meditation, depending on individual suitability and liking.

There is explosion of knowledge in each field. To try learning too many things and participating in so many activities is the present pattern that diverts our mind. We spend lot of time in socializing. This makes us exhausted and burn out. Learn to prioritize and spend time for activities that help you to move ahead in life happily. It is difficult to acquire each piece of knowledge on each and every aspect. At times, we drain our energy in diverting too much and trying to acquire knowledge on subjects that do not have any direct linkage to either our profession or to our overall understanding. This may lose focus on important tasks making life more stressful. The desire to outwit others, maintain your superiority, and accumulate too much information often diverts your limited resources, and may not help in concentrating on your key role. We have a limited time at our disposal; it is prudent to concentrate on only to those activities that are perceived to be helpful. The onset of concentration is to train mind to think and perform one task at a particular time. Concentration is also impacted by long hours of work and fatigue.

Listening to others and taking some time to respond helps in dealing with the issue more effectively. We develop capability to concentrate when not in panic about each and every situation. Let us concentrate on the issue one by one and devote sufficient time to deal with it and not distract mind towards so many other issues.

CHAPTER THIRTY-TWO

SINCERITY

Sincerity will come when we feel inner feelings ought to be reflected in our deeds. We do not want to do double talk. On one side we may express our feelings of love and concern for others, but at the same time hide, deceive or mistrust them. This causes much damage in our effort to remain at calm and in peace than true reflection of feelings towards other people.

Being sincere means to do what we believe. Let actions are dictated by our inner feelings. If we do not like someone and have felt disturbed by his or her actions, let us not behave to show false good feelings. Better to get rid of hidden negative emotions. This needs lot of reformation within to be sincere with someone who troubles us and often gives pain.

It is the sincerity that helps to move ahead in life, with less of internal turmoil. If we are sincere in dealing with others and do what we believe, it will be reflected in our actions. In such case, dealings will be filled with feelings of love and compassion, and actions will reflect inner feelings. It is to respond in a positive manner; as a consequence life will be less tense. Cleverness and tact may help us at times, but it may not be helpful in bringing long lasting calmness. To do what we mean and mean what we do reflects sincerity.

As we develop capability to remain sincere, we will not resort to false concern towards others but try to sort issues. It will bring harmony and better understanding with other person. We will be rid of so much negative emotions leading to peaceful disposition towards others. We will have to express our feelings to the other person, without offending so that they appreciate about our genuine concern. It may be difficult initially, but in the long term, other person will trust you for sincerity and compassion.

Sincerity helps in two ways. One of the benefits of remaining sincere is that there is no conflict between what you do and what you feel. It makes us better placed to be in communication with inner self (consciousness), and do not feel having cheated any one by false talk. We feel troubled when something is done contrary to our consciousness. Sincerity has to do with our inner consciousness. Our inner consciousness is dictated by being in oneness with others as all others are representative of that consciousness. We may make false claim and fool other people, but it gives us pain inside by working contrary to our consciousness. If we move in life with sincere feelings, it provides us satisfaction irrespective of how other people treat us. Sincerity is more helpful for own benefit, as any action that is in harmony with inner consciousness creates less conflict.

At times, we are faced with adverse and negative vibes. We face trouble all round, be it in relation and work situation, and are tempted to adopt manipulative practices. People around us may be selfish and manipulative in pushing things in their favour. Under these situations, it is better to look to good values coming out of inner consciousness. People often get sway with the trend. However, based on strong inner feeling directs people to remain sincere in their dealings for own peace. It is the sincerity in life that provides satisfaction having played role to the best of our capability. This satisfaction derives peace and calmness. It may be possible to impress others through good talk and tact, but in the long run it is the sincere feelings that help to move ahead in peace and happily.

CHAPTER THIRTY-THREE

SELF-ESTEEM

Low self -esteem is common with most people. It is partly self-imposed regardless of original causes; it is due to discounting our capabilities relative to others. This is because the more we criticize ourselves the worse we feel. We lose peace on small provocation due to self-esteem. To be at peace, feel good about yourself; feel that you are worthy as person. The key to good self- esteem is to become aware of personal strengths and recognizing yourself as worthy person despite any real weaknesses.

Finding fault with everything around us is not helpful, except it provides some immediate escape mechanism, but impacts self –esteem. People have a tendency to discount their strengths and good qualities because they find it easy to do, come natural to them, seems like nothing special. The things done by us easily do come natural to us out of personal strengths and qualities. Low self-esteem is likely to affect confidence and motivation to undertake any activity. We become conscious of failures and do not work to our full capability. We lose respect from others, when we fail to respect self in front of others. People prefer not to appreciate our strengths.

Let us build self- esteem by focusing on strengths and not to amplify limitations. Everyone has certain weakness and we are not the only one with some limitation. To build self-esteem, help others in whatever way feel capable. Being a good listener is one way to develop a sense of being good at something and a greater sense of self-worth.

It is important to find how we respond to various situations. People who have high self-esteem will like to prove themselves better; their high esteem makes them to act in more disciplined manner. We like self-esteem to be pampered, feel happy if someone talks highly about us, and thinks much more than we actually deserve. This enhances self-esteem and makes us feel satisfied. People who are otherwise very good and performing better feel their self-esteem affected when they compare their self with someone who is one step above in ladder. It makes them feel inferior.

Self-esteem gets affected by looking to your possessions and achievements. Women who do not perceive themselves as beautiful are low in their self-esteem. They feel inferior in comparison to others. Lack of material possessions affects self-esteem. The modern culture puts premium on beauty, success and material possessions. To remain at peace, it needs more than material comforts. Think that how good you are as a person irrespective of your possessions. Are you able to be good to others? This ought to boost self-esteem.

Take care of self-esteem of other person; it can make that person happy. Those who are junior to us need to be loved and their work recognized to help them to enhance their self-esteem and make them happy. This will do much wonder than mere financial package. People whose self-esteem is low are defensive. They hunger for approval from other persons. We have to take care of these aspirations of the other person. People can contribute significantly to the overall happiness of others by taking care of all these aspects of human relationship. It could be through proper understanding of other person's feelings, worries and genuine appreciation of his/her virtues.

DIFFERENCES

We have to understand inevitability of differences between two people while working together in job or in a relationship. It will be too childish to accept that your views will always be respected. Every aspect of life has different dimensions. Tolerating differences is to know different perspectives. A person who is not able to think broad takes differences as an attempt to undermine his ego and self-respect. People take simple things or different view point personally, and go to any extent to defend self. They do not like other person to clearly present his views. They do not like to take differences with opponents in a positive manner.

It is for our peace and calmness not to make differences with others as a prestige issue. This spoils health as we feel angry, dissociated and hurt when take these differences seriously. Maturity is reflected in our capacity to tolerate differences with others. People who tolerate differences with other people are more likeable;

they derive respect; and able to communicate effectively and find better acceptance from other people.

Our ego is affected and superiority is challenged when required to tolerate differences. This is usually true with some bosses who do not like to listen to different point of view from their subordinates. They feel threatened and make all efforts to challenge ordinary differences. The problem with such people is that they will find it difficult to connect with other people, and to share good and bad feelings and experiences.

Much of our happiness depends on how we remain close to other people. Intolerance makes us to remain aloof with people whether it is at work place or in home. Relations in family and with friends suffer when people are not able to tolerate differences with others. A person who is finding it difficult to tolerate others will rarely find opportunity to laugh, and the happiness generated in sharing other's feelings will be missing.

Let us find whether we are neglecting our personal, spiritual, creative, emotional, or social needs because being busy with job. In such situation, need is to find some time to recharge. With fast track life style and unstable priorities, it is becoming difficult for us to tackle our anger, frustrations, disappointments, grudges and self-created distances from others. Our society often adores people who are aggressive and not likely to tolerate differences.

Even if we are calm person by nature, it is still better to learn to tolerate others is a way to gain positive energy. When we increase our ability to handle the little irritants in life inevitably, we become better equipped to handle the big issues with confidence and inner strength. Differences will be inevitable in our dealings with other person; it is understanding of the real issues and ignoring trivial issues, and adopting a policy of reconciliation without compromising on our core values. It will help in reducing differences and conflict.

We have to understand that loosing tolerance makes us to miss real issue leading to misunderstanding with others. Being tolerant means giving time to think about how to deal with other person more rationally and logical. Intolerance creates quick negative emotions affecting understanding of the actual issue. The inner connection that comes with spirituality prepares for being better tolerant. The feeling of love overpowers any differences.

CHAPTER THIRTY-FIVE

WORRIES

Worry puts strain on both mental and physical health. It leads to anxiety and becomes self-perpetrating with onset of negative thoughts. Worrying about something happening wrong impacts peace of mind and takes away happiness. These worries may not be completely ill founded. We find someone facing problems, and worry that it may also happen to us. We worry about safety of family members, our health, possessions and all these fears haunt us. Negative feelings generally stems from deep-seated fears. Those fears come from a sense of insecurity. It is love that gives a sense of serenity, a psychological and spiritual foundation from which to meet everyone and every circumstance in a positive and constructive way.

It is not always possible to protect completely from uncertainties of future. It is expected of everyone to take normal precautions from natural calamity and pain and injury inflicted by others. When we fear something bad happening, it is better to pray to God for protection as it brings calmness. We believe in the justice of Ultimate and seek strength to face any difficulty.

People who have faced great tragedies on account of death of near one, chronic illness, financial loss or certain wrong allegations have found lot of resilience against these difficulties and faced it with courage. Every misfortune brings enough strength to face it. We know it from our own life experience that when faced with problems, how we have been able to activate our self to meet these challenges.

As we fear of some unknown happening, it is preferable to avoid it while taking usual precaution to protect own and near ones from such eventualities. The complacent attitude towards safety of self and our dear ones could be damaging. We are expected to take adequate steps to protect self and others, without getting unduly worried. The trust and dependence with God takes much of fear and worry from our life. Misfortunes and pain help us to remain in remembrance of God. People faced with difficulties in life establish better faith in the justice of God. They believe in supreme power that energizes them to face challenges of life.

Some of the fears are unfounded and nothing can be done to predict uncertainties in future. Remaining in constant fear and worry does not help us in any way to protect from any adverse happenings. When faced with any crisis, it depends on courage, determination, faith and support at that moment of time that can help in meeting these challenges. A person can avoid fear by developing adequate faith and courage. To be in constant fear is to take away permanent peace of mind.

One has to be prepared to face difficulties and uncertainties of future. Realize that being worried will dampen efforts and will create more worry. It is better to take time and list all the issues that worries and troubles us. We can then plan how to overcome these and possible solutions. Some of the worries may be overcome by hard work and seeking support from others. If we are worried about some past tragedy, better to engage mind in more positive activities to distract out of such situation. It can also be tackled by taking proactive action. Look to other people how they overcome difficult situation. Each person will have to find ways to deal with it, as no uniform solution will work for every individual. This way one can regain peace.

CHAPTER THIRTY-SIX

PROACTIVE

Acting proactively instead of reacting will not only make most situations easier to navigate, it will also help plan for and understand long-term goals. It also enables more flexibility by thinking about the situation in advance, to choose the best option or resolution early on rather than being forced to do something at the last minute which may then be only option. Proactive people tend to be more relaxed, prepared, and positive due to the precautionary steps that they have taken for potential situations. They have more control over their future.

Being Reactive usually forces to take situations as they are and to fix them with minimal time and resources. Decisions are usually made without sufficient understanding of the facts and circumstances resulting in the potential for more problems. Contrary to proactive people, reactive people are usually unorganized, unprepared, and frantic since they usually do not consider the possibility of unexpected situations.

In order to remain at peace and calm, it needs proactive action on various issues that we may encounter. It is to coming out of comfort zone to make things work. To see the big picture, understand there are things that need to be done now to ensure we stay on track with long-term goals. Sometimes, this means trying something new. Being Proactive, it helps in self- improvement as we realize things that need to be given priority for remaining close to core values. We get sufficient time to discover our self and take actions accordingly. We may find some activities not worth pursuing as they may not be in line with long term aspirations. As we become proactive in dealing with situations, it helps in introspection what is good for us to remain in peace. It is important to consider ultimate goal. There will always be little things to worry about, but let us not get bogged in all these things and look to a broader picture. Being Proactive gives opportunity to prioritize and look for these issues in more prepared manner. It gives opportunity for organizing, planning and implementation of the task. It thus augurs well to avoid developing stress situation, onset to life of peace and satisfaction.

Being proactive gives flexibility and confidence to deal with the situation. It helps in anticipating the challenges as sufficient time is available to consider various options. In work environment, reactive employee barely meet deadlines or always feel like falling behind. When this happens the amount of workload piles up, and such employees barely fully meet schedules. Therefore, reactive people never have enough time to assess or review work carefully because of concern trying to just complete tasks and move onto the next thing.

A Proactive employee are in control and prepared for any obstacles. He is able to guide others with the organizing and planning skills developed by being proactive in understanding the issue. This allows him to self-reflect and become an even better employee. You see where you excel and you see what things take more time, allowing you to prepare ahead even more. When we are proactive, we know what the days ahead consist of. We generally have things completed beforehand and know when things are coming up. We get respect in the office, as are considered reliable and completing workload on time. Similarly, Being Proactive in dealing with personal tasks also brings trust and respect with family members. It helps in enjoying the task and remaining relax and calm.

CHAPTER THIRTY-SEVEN

GOD

Everyone in this world is witness to various natural phenomenon which are beyond our capacity to fully understand or analyse. When we think of planets, oceans, mountains and natural creations, it makes us baffled with these complexities of the universe. Various powers of creation and destruction through weather changes, storms, cyclones and earthquakes affect all of us. Science has tried to unravel part of the mystery lying in this natural phenomenon. As we try to know various forces affecting our existence, it becomes clear that some super power is guiding our course of life. We think HIM to be God or divine energy.

A power that guides and controls our existence is not fully known through scientific knowledge. People out of abundant faith in scientific invention tend to believe that what is not known by science is non-existent. This creates doubt in our mind about God and difficulty in finding HIM. Despite these difficulties, it is logical to think of God or divine energy. It satisfies our curiosity to explain mysteries in life. It is the need to seek purpose of life and search for reality. We go to various places to find HIM but the path is often unknown. There is no map or well defined direction that can guide us to reach to God.

To make people to know God, religions have tried to create an image of God in the minds of people as one who is residing in a far off place, may be in Heaven with mighty powers. People therefore try to search for God at various places, may be in heaven, mountains and religious places. We have to understand that God has created us; HIS essence is lying within us. Instead of searching God outside and treating HIM as someone different, it is better to search HIM within. Here we wish to find God, but are not fully aware about HIS likings. As parents, we like our children to love and like each other. Likewise, God will like us to generate love for all other human beings, treat everyone with care, not to generate hate and other negative emotions. We will feel the essence of God only when we bring feeling of love within us.

God is a divine energy, eternal and all pervading. Our soul is a spark of this divine energy. Divinity in the form of inner self (soul) is within us but we do not recognize it. The essence of God lies in realizing this infinite energy. It will be too foolish to think of God as finite. All his actions point towards God being infinite. Our soul is also a spark of that infinite energy. Mentally, we have to think of God as a pure infinite source of energy. Then it does not make sense to search God in heaven. How can someone who is infinite remain at one place and not at the other place? How can God be with one person and not with other person? How can God be outside us but not within us? This logically tells that God is both within you and also outside you. He is everywhere.

Having realized that best way to find God is within, we will feel HIM everywhere, in times of enjoyment and difficulties, in our thought process and actions, while interacting with others and when alone, in our dreams and aspirations. HE will be with us and we will notice inner dialogue all the time with HIM; it will keep us on right path, all our fears and worries will be HIS. We look to all other people as reflection of God; feeling of love flows towards others. In the course of finding God, we acquire the ability of going within and gaining access to the Bliss from our soul. The other way to find God outside may often be misleading.

HELP

One of the cardinal principles of preserving peace is that you help others through love, compassion, better understanding, tolerance and sacrifice. Helping others brings us peace and calmness. It enhances our Self – Esteem by seeing our self-helping others. We look our self as useful, possessing good values and worthy of appreciation. This becomes our perception of self.

Secondly, our inner need is to remain associated with others through love and compassion. We are fulfilling this need. The benefit of helping others and seeing them happy is that it generates a pleasant atmosphere to see all the people around us happy. It multiplies happiness. Other people will in return also try to make us happy through their gratitude. Hence, if we want to be at peace and satisfied, let us try to help others in whatever manner. It will divert our attention from own problems and make us cheerful and filled with joy.

It is worth to notice the satisfaction we derive by providing a small help to the other person. Despite physical discomforts, such acts of helping others enhance self-esteem. It is not possible to be able to create calmness by being completely isolated from others. If we help other person in whatever small manner, like showing a person a particular direction, helping old person to cross road, helping child to move; we feel good and useful in our own judgment.

You can adopt helping attitude in whatever small manner; be it at work or at home with your family. Let us behave with others in a manner that is devoid of fault finding. Talk on issues that is understood and liked by others. Be sensitive to know about other persons' problems. Do not compare other person with better performer. Talk of his/her achievements. Our own achievements and successes may not be of much interest to others unless we take sufficient interest in their welfare.

To help others is to show words of kindness, understanding, love and compassion while talking to them. This behaviour is in tune with inner self and it makes us feel better and happy. It removes conflict and stress. To show words of kindness to others does a great wonder. Many successful people have adopted this trait to attract people; draw their attention and make them feel better. Helping others is the most effective way to bring positivity in our action and behaviour. However, it should not boost ego and superiority complex. It is to be observed whether such acts help the person to regain peace and calmness. A person who is helping others have to realize that nature has also been kind to him in so many ways and this act of helping others is to repay.

To be helpful and kind to someone is difficult; because we either feel that the person does not deserve or we remain irritated and angry with his attitude. Being kind to someone who is better placed compared to us is not sufficient. That person may not require your kindness and good words. Let us provide kindness to someone who feels happy with it. To be at peace and happy in isolation is short lived. If all other people are tense and worried, it is difficult to feel joy and happiness. It is in own interest to make the entire atmosphere feel lively and joyous through helping others and being kind. Helping attitude does a lot good to the well-being of others, and in return brings us peace and satisfaction.

HAPPINESS

Our attitude towards life depends on intention to remain happy. We cannot bring long lasting peace unless intention is to remain happy. It depends on how important we feel to remain happy. It may look opposite to being serious, dedicated and committed. It occurs to so many people that to be happy is not everything in life as other attributes like sincerity to work, higher goals in life and service to mankind are more important.

Happy people may look to be casual in approach, not hardworking, spending time in wasteful luxuries and not serious in pursuit of their duties. People who attach these negative attributes to happiness may not feel intense desire to be happy. They may not work hard to derive happiness from the activities performed by them, and look for other people to provide them feeling of happiness. It is up to each individual to feel need to be happy and seek it through own efforts, without depending on somebody else to make us happy. Nobody will be able to make you happy unless you yourself wish to cheer up.

Thinking is more tuned towards facing the hardships of life and thus lose desire and intention to be happy. We lack inner transformation to move towards happiness, till we deem it to be casual approach to life. The happiness has to flow within by being responsible and not to blame others for making us feel depressed.

It is common practice to blame and put responsibility on others for our worries and difficulties. If the boss is a cause of your unhappiness, you could make efforts to make boss happy by your work or ignore the difficulties faced while dealing with the boss and maintain calmness. People try to defend actions and justify being in unhappy condition by proclaiming helplessness and difficulties.

The choice to be happy varies from person to person. We have to search happiness from things we like most without imitating others. Having once identified things that make us happy, it is desirable to pursue these activities. It is found to be difficult at times to find enough time to devote to activities and our hobbies for creating happiness. People create some interest in pursuing activity like listening to music, walking, outdoor activities, meeting friends or any other activity to remain busy with enjoyable experiences.

Unhappy people generally do not maintain any agenda for creating happiness. It is difficult for such people to derive happiness from day to day events. It is important to think of creating happiness from what we do in a day to day life. Special occasions like generating high profits, success in job, promotions in career or favourable situation may not come on a regular basis. If we wait for such occasions to be happy, it will keep us waiting and over thinking for such occasions.

Happiness also comes by appreciation all the good things that come in our journey of life, and feeling good about our own self, enjoying what we have accomplished, our personality, our job, our belongings etc. Happiness is thus a full time activity. With every step towards happiness brings a state of calmness and peace pervading all around.

CHAPTER FORTY

SIMPLICITY

Life is complex in nature and it needs special efforts to remain simple and calm. Knowledge on various fields is vast, and special efforts are needed to acquire it. Jobs have become complex and stressful. Various complicated and sophisticated gadgets are available in the market for use at home and office; costly and modern vehicles for comfortable journey and lavish home to live.

It requires us to work hard to excel in profession so as to amass wealth; acquire material possessions; enjoy and spend time in using these gadgets, and then to protect all these belongings from damage and theft. There is nothing wrong in acquiring comfortable lifestyle, as long we keep our desires and expectations under control. We have to re-examine whether it augurs well to carry on complex life style. However, the entire process of hankering for complicated life style, enjoy the comforts that come with it, preserving this life style puts lot of pressure on our time and resources. Present lifestyle puts too much pressure on our health and time to amass and use or misuse all these belongings.

People who wish to develop in inner essence feel urge to remain simple in outward appearance. Mind does not get distracted to undesirable lifestyle; it is to preserve inner peace and calmness by being simple. In a limited human life span, people miss the happiness derived from simple and easily available possessions in the search for more complicated things. This is the unfortunate situation in the present competitive world.

It is however for own good to think whether all these complexities are worth accumulating. Are we not comfortable with good and simple food, simple living and good attitude? Are we not making others feel bad and small by adopting complexities in our lifestyle? Let us be simple in our attitudes, possessions, eating habits, expectations, language and behaviour. We will be able to communicate with people with the feeling of love, if able to maintain simplicity in dealings with others. Being simple means that you shed ego and to not expect too much from external world. The simple lifestyle will be possible if we feel absorbed for some time with our inner self. This will make us not to get distract with outside complexity in life.

Being simple in life is to pursue all our needs without

getting too much panicky. Truth in life is better understood when we are humble, simple and contented. When simple, we fill the need of our body and that of inner soul. Eliminate all the possessions which have no significant value to our enrichment.

The problem is that anything simple is treated as outdated and old. If simple thing serves our purpose, still market will be flooded with more costly products. The temptation to adopt complex life style, due to the vigorous advertising and marketing campaign, needs to be curtailed. It is up to each individual what he wishes to derive from his life. If the ultimate goal is to generate long lasting peace and happiness, one has to be simple in attitude. Even if a wealthy person has all the comforts available, he has to be simple in his life style, and not to impact his inner calmness with hectic lifestyle.

CHAPTER FORTY-ONE

INTEGRITY

Integrity means practicing what one believes is right. A 'man of principle is not a man who understands a principle, but a man who understands, accepts, and lives by a principle. Integrity is an internal system of principles which guides our behaviour. Integrity is a choice rather than an obligation. Integrity cannot be forced by outside sources.

When we are acting with integrity, we do what is right, even when no one is watching. People of integrity are guided by a set of core principles that empowers them to behave consistently to high standards. The core principles of integrity are virtues, like compassion, dependability, generosity, honesty, kindness, loyalty, maturity, objectivity, respect, trust and wisdom. Virtues are the valuable personal and professional resources which people develop and use these to work. We talk often about integrity and emphasize it as a quality, but have a narrow perspective of how the man of integrity is expected to deal with other person.

The important reason to practice one's beliefs is that if it is right, it benefits our own life. Any deviation from what we know to be right is an attack on own belief. To act contrary to own knowledge is accepting the premise that integrity is different from self-interest, and that bypassing integrity will somehow make life better. Instead of seeing morality as a tool for survival, we see it as a restriction that makes life more difficult. Every act that violates integrity weakens the moral habit, until our emotions are unaligned with our thoughts.

A man who practices what he preaches is predictable, and few will feel threatened by him. Trust can develop, since others will come to realize you are consistently virtuous. To act without integrity, even occasionally, is to make others feel distrustful. This can negatively impact one's life in a number of ways. People will not allow themselves to become emotionally close to you. They will always fear your betrayal.

What is it that holds people from adopting integrity in their dealings with others? It is own weakness. Adopting integrity is the most preferred virtue. We have to overcome weakness so as to move close to being a person of integrity. First, let us not advise, offer suggestions and expect something from others which we are not able to do our self. The best way to command respect is to lead by example. If a person wishes others to be disciplined, try to enforce same level of discipline on self. If someone is undergoing through difficult problem, try to place yourself in that situation and show adequate empathy rather than offering suggestions. A man of integrity believes in real action rather than advices. He will prefer not to hide his weakness and magnify his virtues.

It is difficult for most of us to adopt this virtue to be part of personal values. Still, there are ample moments in day to day life where without losing anything, we can bring integrity in our dealings with other people. Let us talk straight and do not either glorify or underestimate anything. Learn to respect others. It is preferable to speak what we believe without offending others. Start with simple acts of integrity, it will reinforce in our value system. A person will be truly man of integrity when he has courage to stand by truth and righteous irrespective of personal gain or loss. It is a step towards creating meaning and value in life. It will eventually bring peace and satisfaction in life.

CHAPTER FORTY-TWO

TRUST

People who are sincere and show sense of responsibility are able to create an environment of trust. If someone perceives you a man of truthfulness and sincere, it changes the underlying causes that created situation of mistrust. Everyone creates either an environment of trust or mistrust. It is not appropriate to blame the external environment and other people; we are also partly responsible for creating situations that bring mistrust, onset of conflict, jealousy and troubles. The other way to improve trust is to trust others with the hope that eventually others will also develop trust in you.

If there is mistrust in our dealings with others, it pollutes entire atmosphere. People will not believe us. People ought to trust our words and feel comfortable while discussing any problem. It is a step towards attaining better values of life. If people perceive you trustworthy, they feel interconnected with you. It will be much more rewarding than any other tangible thing.

It is difficult to develop trust without believing about the goodness of other people. If we feel that every other person is cheat, with such a bent of mind makes it extremely difficult to trust someone. True, we might have some bad experiences while dealing with people, but does that ought to haunt to make us to lose trust. We learn the lessons of life by developing trust. Even if we get stuck and cheated on certain occasions, still it generates a positive outlook to life.

Developing trust in a society helps in creating a flexible environment where people can get what they need from others at a time when they need, and repay back at a future date when they have the capability and resources. Trust is developed from the belief that eventually if you be good to someone it will be repaid back in some way or the other. Trust is an attitude and a belief that drives people to believe others. There may be instances where we find someone not trustworthy, looking to his past dealings, but it ought not to make us feel jittery to trust people. Developing trust is ideal to improve activities at work place through better coordination and delegation of work. Juniors who are not trusted find it difficult to perform efficiently. Trust is antidote to maintain good relations. It will be difficult to move ahead in life, with mistrust most of the people with whom we interact. The other person in turn also mistrusts us, the entire environment remains suspicious; impacting love, compassion and empathy.

Trust creates a strong bondage that is based on honesty and fair dealings. How many times we talk about positive attitude, good behaviour and better communication with others. The best way to communicate with others is to create environment of trust. In such situation, blaming, accusing and hostility do not exist. Trust has a great healing power that resolves problems and issues by giving strength to forgiveness, understanding and healthy communication.

Look to people who are not able to trust others, it makes them jittery to show compassion towards others. Developing trust is to feel connected with other people; it is in tandem with reality of our existence, losing it is to go against the flow of life. Let us make some exceptions as not to trust someone who is likely to cheat us, but as a general rule, let us learn to trust others. Look to family relations; lack of trust is the root cause of troubles, misunderstandings and suffering. Look to business dealings which are impacted by mistrust. We suffer lot in developing cordial relations with our spouse and relations in an environment of mistrust.

HONESTY

Honesty advocates doing all the activities based on fair dealing without cheating anyone. So, basically, honesty means giving a value to truth. If one acknowledges his mistakes, if one never tells a lie, if one is true to someone, the person can be called 'an honest person'. A person will be honest if he thinks about wellbeing of others as important as his own. He prefers not to gain in importance and stature, both professionally and materially by taking undue advantages and harming the interest of others. He is interested in a level playing field. Honesty will be reflected in his dealings with other people. He will prefer not to do double talk; avoid talking something while meaning and doing contrary to it.

People in the present cut throat competitive world often do all sort of acts in a more professional manner to grow by putting breaks and hurdles on their peers and immediate competitors. This is mostly not reflected and known to others; however, the person doing it may be aware about these tactics adopted to further his self-interest at the cost of others. We may not treat such people as dishonest but they are not either honest in the true sense of word. People generally have a narrow conception of honesty. It suits most people to interpret honesty to be revealing truthfulness when it does not affect them adversely.

People give the impression of being honest and sophisticated in behaviour, try to be good at communication and possess convincing abilities, but inner feelings may be far away from honesty. It is therefore difficult to find a person who is truly honest. A person, who does not cheat, and also tells truth, but being in a position of advantage make others to suffer. Hence honesty is not only confined to being truthful, but has much to do with moral ethics.

Honesty, at times, has the ability to cause misfortune to the person who displays it. There are dishonest people and they like to take advantage of an honest person. An honest person finds it difficult to understand such tactics; he feels uncomfortable and dismayed to deal with such people. He feels need to be careful and cautious in taking favours and socializing with others; otherwise, he may fall into wrong trap.

Adopting honesty traits have to come in a gradual manner. This needs self-introspection at regular intervals. First, it is important to realize that everything happening around us need not to be viewed in the context of gain or loss. If something is good in life, it ought to be perceived irrespective of any tangible benefits from it. It is too narrow to look to everything in terms of material benefits. Once we shed these apprehensions, it helps us to adopt the acts of honesty with firm conviction.

Sacrifices that an honest person makes to remain bound to his ideals often get unnoticed. A truly honest person knows that real essence of life lies in listening to inner consciousness. It provides inner calmness. After, lot of success, achievement and fame, the ultimate thing that each individual ought to aspire is inner peace. The sacrifices that we make to be an honest person are worth the benefits it can serve to develop inner strength. As people realize inner consciousness, they will move close to the honesty. Inner consciousness comes out of feelings of divine or soul within. The ultimate purpose of life ought to be to connect with inner consciousness, honesty is that trait to take us to realize it. It is a process of self-discovery.

CHAPTER FORTY-FOUR

EGO

Ego is that state of awareness which thinks of you as separate from the other person. Being separate makes us to think about our achievement, success, failure, troubles, fears and hopes. Ego is identifying you as different from others. This type of Ego is good to enable that the person is able to act in a responsible manner due to this self-esteem. However, a person who carries too much of ego is always busy in identifying himself as separate and in the process loses his real identity, that being oneness with the other people. Ego comes out of self-consciousness which describes a person distinct from other persons. However, inner consciousness which is also God consciousness reflects connection with other persons. Too much of self-consciousness at the cost of ignoring inner-consciousness creates selfish tendencies.

Ego is self-identity and discovers individual qualities as distinct from others. As we remove all these qualities that distinguishes us from others, we find 'pure we' and the 'pure other' are one and the same, there has always been only one existence, call it the One, or the Soul, or God.

Ego is desirable to enable a person to maintain his identity and to prove worthy. The foremost quality of ego is self-preservation. However, in maintaining separate identity, one goes too far to consider self as separate from other individual, and develops the urge to outwit, compete and fight with other person. We try to impose onto others around us, that is where the problem comes and conflict arises. We define as somebody now, and want to preserve this definition of our self into the future till we understand self. Similarly, when we try to impose our definition to others, the 'other' ego resists it and there comes a conflict.

Inner consciousness works in harmony. In reality, there is only one, the pure existence, consciousness, bliss absolute. It's not 'my' existence or 'my' consciousness or 'your' consciousness, but it's THE consciousness. This awareness acts harmoniously. Think of so many things that connect you with other person. It does not undergo change.

Much of the problems in today's world are somewhat directly or indirectly related to the ego within our self.

An egoistic person is driven by the perceptions in their head, and not the feelings in their heart. Such person expect others to fall in line with his thinking and does not respect divergent views. It becomes difficult to work with egoistic person because of these traits. As we think too much about our identity, it pushes up ego and makes us worried about achievements and success in life. Ego is desirable when kept within limit as it will encourage us to be distinct, excellent and outperform others. This provides purpose of life. However, often people get bogged down too much with their personal achievements and enhance their ego levels to such an extent that they miss their real self. Life is a journey and at the end, neither success nor failure is of any significance. Your individual identity will be merged with the identity of others. Hence, personal ego is a temporary phenomenon to maintain separate identity, for a definite purpose. Personal ego has to eventually merge with Pure Ego and efforts ought to be in that particular direction. Pure Ego or inner consciousness does not need any preservation, because it knows itself to be only existence. The truth is that all temporary things ought to be treated as a passing phase in life.

CHAPTER FORTY-FIVE

SATISFACTION

It is not adequate to base our satisfaction alone on external possessions. First, we do not have full control on these and it may take a long time to acquire but limited time to enjoy it. Secondly, the moment we acquire something, the desire for something else is created. Bringing overall satisfaction demands that we also look to so many intangible things in life. These intangibles are Love, Honesty, Empathy and Compassion, but are not emphasised. Adopt right approach to life based on overall concern for the people with whom you are living and generosity in dealing with others. These qualities create a positive environment and a lively atmosphere which simple material possessions lack.

The achievement of such goals as wealth, beauty and fame do not bring long lasting satisfaction. It can only be achieved if a person grows as an individual, maintains strong relationships with their loved ones and be compassionate towards others. Those who restrict to material benefits are more likely to experience negative emotions, such as anger, ailments and lethargy. At the same time, people who aspire beyond material comforts are more physically fit, feel more positive, keep strong social relationships with their close ones and experience less stress.

While a person ought to work hard to earn and be better placed professionally, but let it not become entire source of your satisfaction in life. This mistake is committed by so many people who overemphasize such type of satisfaction in a world which is filled with materialistic advancement.

People have to learn to be satisfied by looking not only for own satisfaction but of satisfaction of others. It cannot be an isolated event. The more we work to bring satisfaction to others will make the environment peaceful. By assisting others and identifying your personal strengths and then consciously incorporating those into daily activities will bring greater happiness and life satisfaction. Consciously identifying your unique strengths and embracing them as something that makes you unique and special will help you appreciate these special abilities.

Finally, satisfaction in life comes by engaging in activities that provides you enjoyment, happiness and appreciation. Every person has certain inherent strengths to be useful in the life. He can be creative. Using that strength can bring satisfaction by being talented and creative. There are countless ways a person can express their creativity and each one of them brings intense satisfaction and fulfilment. The best thing to feel satisfied with is to love self and believe in own capability. One ought to look useful in his own judgment. It depends on how to adopt good values, and curtail activities that may provide temporary joy but are damaging in the long period.

Satisfaction has not to do with mere achievement. It is a state of mind. Engaging in activities that are interesting, adopting positive attitude and remaining connected with other people offer satisfaction. People have to create satisfaction in what he is, what he does and what he believes. Your life ought to look meaningful to you to be satisfied with it. The path to satisfaction is to realize true self and to be closely connected with inner consciousness. The state of satisfaction is closely related to level of peace and calmness.

CHAPTER FORTY-SIX

ACTIONS

Everyone knows that some actions can be certainly good or bad. Going further, it may look too baffling to know that what is good at first sight may turn out to have different perspective on further interpretation. How many times, we discover as true has been proven wrong. In this process, we misunderstood other person and disregard other person's view. Except for certain moral values, there is nothing like good and bad action.

Good actions ought to increase overall prosperity and happiness while bad actions undermine those values. However, most actions are matter of preference and cannot be deemed as good or bad, despite certain actions never change their basic attribute as either good or bad action. Universally good or bad actions are objectively based on the truth that anything which protects life and dignity of human beings is a good action. But other actions cannot be judged in terms of good or bad because they are a matter of personal preference determined by individual attitudes.

There are certain moral values and nobody have any argument on these values being right for the person. Love, Honesty, Sincerity and Commitment are life enriching attitudes that brings calmness, peace and happiness not to self but all other people around us. These morals are not determined by anyone. Leaving behind moral and real issues in life that differentiate what is good and bad, everything else in life cannot be described in terms of good and bad actions.

There are host of activities which are responses to the demand at a particular time. Something good at a particular moment may not look good for all the time. Someone wishes to be happy and casual in life while other person remains more serious. Both these attitudes to life have definite advantageous. Remaining serious all the time brings stress and expectations. Casual approach in life may at times affect you by losing available opportunities. We have been taught to accomplish a task in a particular manner, and if someone does the same thing differently, it prompts us to find fault in other person.

Most emotions, activities and responses cannot be branded as good or bad activities. There is nothing good or bad in doing a particular act. It is a relative comparison and best way to describe these 'more' or 'less' in comparison to other activity. Love and hate are often treated as good and bad activities. Similarly honesty and dishonesty are opposites and thought to be good and bad activities. It does not work like that in life. A person, who is seen to hate others, is actually showing less of love compared to other person. He may still be lovable in comparison to third person. Similarly, honesty is a relative comparison and nobody is fully honest or dishonest. It is not possible for us to have analysis of what is good or bad action for other person.

People often review various actions taken by others, and spend lot of time in judging others. It burdens us with emotions, without understanding what action is good and bad for other person. These judgments are our subjective opinion. A completely different opinion is held by some other person. It is therefore imperative to not sit on judgment of others on issues which are subjective in nature. We may be by doing so hurting other person and losing our peace of mind.

CHAPTER FORTY-SEVEN

MULTI-TASKING

The mind can focus on one thought or one action at a time. When we do several things at the same time, we are actually moving our attention quickly from one thought or object to another, and it only seems to us that we are focusing on several tasks at the same time. Multitasking can become tiring, and could interfere with completing tasks successfully, as it does not allow to focus on each task. After developing a certain degree of concentration ability, we may be able to hold the mind for longer periods entirely on one subject, and will be able to understand and accomplish the task efficiently.

With a better concentration, it is easier to focus mind on one thing, subject or task, and also easier to handle several tasks at the same time when need arises. Concentration allows to focus attention on one thing at a time, and therefore, acquire better results and carry out everything efficiently. With multi-tasking, it divides our attention, and moves focus from one thing to another, and therefore, likely to lose energy and time, and might do mistakes and errors because not being attentive. People who are not able to cope with multi-tasking remain tense and lose peace of mind.

Improving concentration does not make mind rigid and stubborn. On the contrary, it strengthens and sharpen our senses, enhances intuition, makes mind more peaceful, and helps in many ways. To achieve peace of mind, it is important to remain focus and concentrate on particular task at a time. We can develop concentration even during multi-tasking by not thinking too much on results and rewards. Mind to be dissociated from all these thoughts and try enjoy job and activity going along with it. The more we enjoy and like job will improve concentration and multi-tasking will be easily accomplished. Hence, efforts be not to lose concentration during multi- tasking.

It may not be possible to avoid multi-tasking, but can be managed through proper planning and proactive action. These days' demands of profession expect you to do multi-tasking, it builds pressure and stress. Hence, even during multi-tasking, need is to avoid getting obsessed with so many thoughts at a time, but to concentrate on the activity in which are presently engaged. It requires proper planning to take various activities serially, and shift to other task as per time schedule allotted to each task. The focus improves productivity and time is available to shift to another task. By learning to focus on the task at hand, we learn to do one thing at a time, and move swiftly from one task to another. Learning to keep attention on one thing is outcome of concentration, it disregards and reject unwanted thoughts, and this means greater inner peace and tranquillity. With greater inner peace, we attain greater control of mind and thoughts, and it becomes easier to clear mind from irrelevant thoughts when need is to focus.

Even though, we are supposed to carry out number of tasks at a time, let us not be panic and rush to so many activities at a time. It is possible through proper planning and implementation to direct self and juniors to concentrate on one activity at a time as to not create a situation of stress and panic in work environment. This will help in bringing conducive environment at work place. It helps in restoring peace, while performing multi-tasking by focus on concentration and planning.

CHAPTER FORTY-EIGHT

ACCEPTANCE

The beauty of life is that it is unpredictable. Nothing is permanent, everything changes and lot of things can happen that will transform who we are and have an impact on our life. The problem is that we need to cultivate the ability to truly accept whatever comes and embrace it. Believe that everything happens for a reason and that better things will always follow. That is the beginning of true acceptance. It is hard to practice acceptance when we deeply wish things were different. But the truth is, sometimes we cannot change our fate, even if we try.

Life brings many challenges, such as the death of someone we love, and it is not easy to embrace it and wishing those things would have never happened. But if we start cultivating acceptance in our lives right now, we will likely cope with future crises in a different way and view them from a different perspective. We might want things to be different in the future, but in the present moment we need to accept things as they unfold. That is the way we can make our life flow smoothly instead of roughly.

There are two ways out of a problem: accept what are happening, see the positive, and choose a peaceful state of mind; or fight against it, be miserable, and struggle against the universe. Practicing acceptance prepares us to live in this changing world, where we never know what is going to happen next. Acceptance is like protecting self with our own armour. Acceptance is not at all related to weakness, and is definitely not a substitute of orthodoxy or mediocrity. We need to learn when it is time to persist and when it is time to accept. One thing that makes acceptance much easier is to list all the possible explanations for why we are experiencing something. We are not fully aware about the situation that unfolds, and find it painful at the initial stage, but may be advantageous for us as we deal with the situation.

Whether it is a family loss, a missed opportunity, or a sudden change in our plans, being able to accept things that are out of our control will help maintain inner peace and happiness. As we understand the broad picture of life, it draws on us that we have little control on various happenings. It may not be possible to resolve all the problems. We may feel satisfied in certain situation and dissatisfied with other happenings. To grudge about what is not liked does not do any good. We like to have things to be settled and want explanations for things that we do not understand. This happens in many situations whether at professional level or in relationships. We have thoughts that run through our brains about why we are not getting the response we desire so much. We create stories about why people are not responding in the way we hoped. In doing these things, we can continue down of unanswered questions and hurt feelings.

Muster compassion for someone who hurt you, instead of self-pitying in bitterness, which will make it easier to forgive them and set yourself free. Set aside some time to actively enjoy the good things about the present. Create a list of things you love about yourself instead of dwelling on how you wish you were different. Focus on what you appreciate about the people in your life instead of wishing they would change. We cannot expect the outside world to take care of our feelings. We have to accept this reality. This includes letting go of what others thinks of us, practicing self-validation, knowing that we are worthy. So many feelings come up when we are hurting or feeling rejected.

FAIR DEALINGS

Every person has a choice to make on a daily basis; whether to hold to the highest level of fairness in dealings or to compromise for own benefit. The highest level of fair dealings has to be in essence and not only in appearance. You may boost about acting in a fair manner and claim to be so in front of other person. This is what most of us are trying to do in life. However, there are large number of actions where these are not completely fair dealings, it does not jell with inner self, but outsiders are not aware about it. You know that this is not correct. At the back of our mind is to protect self-interest, fair dealing comes only next to it. To think about welfare of the person with whom we are interacting is the first step to adopt fair dealings. People instead of posing to be acting in a fair manner ought to look within and satisfy that they act in a fair manner. It demands showing equanimity in feelings, sincerity in approach and truthfulness in dealings. The purpose is not to put a person in a disadvantageous position.

Adopting fair dealings are taught at various levels, but it is common to observe dealings that are not fully fair. In business dealings, promises are made but the end product and performance fall short of such promises. In dealing with other person, course of events are twisted so as to suit our needs. People in place of authority often fail to deal fairly with their subordinates. This is due to specific preferences borne out of bias on the basis of culture, caste, region or individual attitude.

The perception that someone is not up to our liking often damages the credibility of that person. Knowingly or unknowingly these impressions are carried by so many people in an organization that destroys the reputation and chances of growth of other person. We fail to give a fair dealing to the other person by adopting such attitude. It is worth to examine whether these attitudes are based on strong facts or out of bias. Look rationally, our attitude towards someone carries some sort of bias. It is largely prevalent in multi-cultural, multi lingual and multi religious societies. People develop certain specific preferences that affect fair dealings with others. Without any reason or data, you make someone suffer. You derive someone his chances to grow, and prefer someone else merely because of some prejudice.

At times, people are not able to understand other person well. He is treated as something different than what he is. These treatment and impression about other person is created both intentional and non-intentional. Sometimes, we feel threatened by colleague who is likely to be our competitor. We try to create a negative impression of that person in front of others. All these tactics are borne out of selfish tendencies so as to put other person in a disadvantage.

In normal day to day life, the tendency is to hide own weakness and expect other person to treat and deal with you without knowing fully about you. People project themselves to be expert, professional and supportive while the actual position may be different. They try to give advices on matters not fully aware about. They will try to talk something to mislead others. People try to gain in importance and respect in an unfair way. Most of the time, these tactics may not be fully revealed, and the person using such means moves on in life. However, it puts burden on the person to hold on to these lies and impacts peace of mind.

CHAPTER FIFTY

OPTIMISM

The advantage of being optimist is that such people have expectation of better future. They pass the present in the hope of the better future. The thought itself generates happiness. They remain less distracted and focus on present moment. This outlook help to remain at peace and satisfied. Even if the future does not unfold any pleasant things, still such people depict positive thoughts about next future event.

Pessimists fear about future problems and they do not perceive any good things happenings around them. People witness both good and bad events. Pessimists amplify negative events and feel helpless. They do not find world worth of enjoying. People who are optimist treat various events of life in a more positive manner. They do not find fault with the situation in which they are placed, rather they enjoy life as it folds before them. Optimists worry less and try to enjoy small things and pleasures surrounding their life.

They socialize more and feel less burnout inside. Much of the optimism comes out of past experiences as also from inborn qualities. There are specific traits of optimists; pleasant ways of thinking that bring them more success, better health, increased life satisfaction, and other rewards on a regular basis. Cultivating the mind of an optimist does not mean pursuing happiness, regardless of circumstance, but it can bring more things into life to be happy.

Let us try to be more optimist than what are at present, by trying to attend to the problem, enjoying the problem and not worrying too much about the end results and failures. People who are depicting optimist behaviour show such type of traits. They take life as it comes and enjoy the events as it folds without getting worried about the end result. If the failure comes on the way, it does not bother them too much. They look for next opportunity in life to succeed. This type of attitude makes the journey of life peaceful and happy. They develop positive energy to accomplish a particular task more effectively. Thinking about better future energizes to reach up to that level by consistent efforts.

A person may be optimist in a particular occasion but pessimist in different situation, based on individual capabilities and past experiences. Optimist looks to his capabilities and feels confident in difficult situations. On the contrary, pessimist is mindful of his weakness, and anticipates worst things to come. People improve their optimism by hoping for good things to come in life, and let this thought be inculcated on a regular basis. Feeling grateful for good things and enjoying better things in life is indication of optimism. Everyone can count on number of blessings in life. This thought process reduces worry and improve optimism and happiness.

Some people wish to do right job, remain helpful, and not to bother too much about end results. This is the philosophy they hold, as core values in life. As we believe in our capabilities and remain less worried about end result, it makes us calm to be engrossed in our role. In such a condition, action derives happiness and not the mere result. This is in tune with spirituality. A person who is optimist feels enjoyment and happiness in his actions. His mind remains more focused on the job and less on end results. Right action eventually generates good results.

LOVE

Feeling love and concern for others is remedy of many negative emotions and is a way to generate long lasting peace and calmness. It ought to become part of our personality and outlook towards others. We may talk nicely to make others happy, but if not supported by sincere feeling will not bring desired warmth. It requires us to be truthful, caring and tolerant when in love with other person. Love is a feeling of well-being for other person. It has a broader dimension and goes much beyond physical intimacy. Love is like an energy that makes us feel good and diverts our mind from bad feelings.

Being in love with others is an activity that is to think good of others and create such environment to make others feel happy. As we take food to nourish our body, sleep to give rest to the body, similarly love brings emotional well-being. Engaging in love is good for emotions; it is better achieved through self-introspection to find whether our actions are directed to bring happiness to other person.

Facing problems is normal with everyone. Getting too much worried with our own self may not help to face the realities of life. It is always better even in the worst of the situations to keep calm. It does not help us to feel panic and worried with the problems of life, as we do not have control on end results which in most cases are dependent on so many factors. Life has not to be made unpleasant by thinking and remaining engrossed in a single activity that affect a well-adjusted life. This impacts generating feeling of love when bogged down with problems.

As people believe to be sophisticated and refined, they find it difficult to connect with other person and judge them to be eligible for their love. They find other person not refined and feel it difficult to love him or her. Love is often treated as bargaining power to generate favours, and most of us do not believe in love as a main goal of life. If we accept some one with his shortcomings unconditionally, unaware of our own troubles and try to make him feel good, it is true love.

Love develops an urge to help other person without expecting anything in return. The feeling of love has to generate in our heart. Creating love within is to understand our true essence. The more we realize inner connection with other people, the better we are to love others. Developing loving feelings is a sign of self-improvement. If heart yearns for love and concern feelings for other person, it reflects our progress on the path of spirituality. This feeling of love has to be universal. You may love your family more than other people, but it need not to remain confined to select few. This divine love is pious than mere physical intimacy. It recharges our soul. Depriving inner self of this subtle feeling of love is to create inner turmoil.

The most important reason for people to be stressed is that they have gradually forgotten to love others. The situation has become so grave that love is now missing in our family and close relationship. It is the cause for constant turmoil, stress and loss of focus in life. Most people despite all the comforts in life are not happy. The reason is that they are not able to connect with the God through the feeling of genuine love for all creations.

CHAPTER FIFTY-TWO

COMPASSION

Compassion is a human emotion prompted by the pain of others. More vigorous than empathy, this feeling commonly gives rise to an active desire to alleviate another's suffering. It is the ability to understand the emotional state of another person. Empathy, as most people know, is the ability to put self in the other person's place. Although compassion and empathy are two separate things, having compassion for someone can generate a feeling of empathy, to understand the pain of other person.

There are so many people in this world who are suffering in some manner. Why to feel concerned about people who suffer. These suffering could be on account of wrong deeds. Do we have the time from own worries to bother about suffering of other person. We find a person in great pain, but walk away without doing anything as somebody else is supposed to take care of that person. This insensitivity to the suffering has grown, and feeling for the pain of others is ignored. When we face the suffering, world comes crushing down on us, and we pray for support from someone. How bad we feel if nobody comes forward for help.

Compassion for others will be generated only when you notice that other person is suffering. If you ignore to notice the suffering of old person, patient, orphanage, widow and economically deprived person, you may not feel compassion for how difficult is their condition. It involves sensitivity so that your heart responds to their pain. Compassion is to suffer along with the other person. When this occurs, you feel warmth, caring, and the desire to help the suffering person in some way. Having compassion also means that you offer understanding and kindness to others when they fail or make mistakes, rather than judging them harshly.

Wealth and Power bring ego and it makes a person to expect everything to happen in the manner he deems it right. The ego takes us far off from understanding the plight of other person. All the people with whom we interact will not reveal their suffering to us. We find it difficult to feel compassion for other person. We find people often saying that we were not aware about the plight of their friend, relative and family members. It does not work like that. Your family member may be suffering some pain but you are not able to feel it. This shows your insensitivity to the suffering of others. If you yourself is feeling troubled, you need to first feel compassion for self before you can show it to others. Sometimes, people due to continuous work pressure, lose compassion and behave angry, burnt out, and exhausted. This feeling comes after too many hard days of work, too many difficult clients and too many unwinnable cases. Under this situation, it may be difficult to feel compassion for others.

Compassion is a feeling to be useful to others, and mitigate their sufferings. If a person forces to be seen as compassionate, it shows that inner self lacks such feelings. The more we tell ourselves to be compassionate, the harder it is, the more internal resistance we feel. Inner self ought to be calm and in peace so as to feel compassionate for others. Our desire for wealth and status ought to be in moderation, leaving sufficient time to understand the plight of others. Compassion is the outcome of inner feelings which get refined with every stage of journey that draws us close to inner consciousness. Every step towards honestly, truth, sincerity and sympathetic makes a person compassionate.

CHAPTER FIFTY-THREE

MEDITATION

Meditation is to control the tendency of the mind to continuously think and search for something pleasurable and appealing. Mind wanders to look for material comforts, boost self ego and to be in competition with others. In the process, mind remains restless and keeps on developing different scenarios, about future plans and past memories. This condition of mind of looking for outward pleasures creates lot of stress.

All along we are being taught to look for happiness and peace from success, material comforts, relations and enjoyment. The mind in the process of doing all that tries to burden itself too much and loses its calmness. The best way to reduce the burden on the mind is to draw its attention from external environment to inward attention through meditation. It will then naturally flow towards more and more inward path, with the mind knowing that by taking this course, it will find what it is looking for, absolute bliss consciousness.

As the mind take this inward route, it is then meditating on what is real and looks at it with deeper levels of consciousness. This absorption of mind to the real essence which is away from involvement in bodily pleasures brings different type of relaxation, which is difficult to know without practice.

It may look too preliminary or rudimentary to shut eyes and relax to make the mind to search for reality. The fact of our existence is that people have gone too far in the direction of materiality that it will need shutting mind and reversing or undoing so as to allow it to think of spiritual essence. Meditation tries to bring to the point where mind achieves the tranquillity to be in still and bliss condition. A person who sits down with the intention to calm down, he has to erase all the problems that impact this condition of stillness.

Meditation is a process where you empty mind from the unwarranted stuff so that it on its own goes towards reality. Mind will not stop thinking. If it stops thinking outside, it will look inside. It looks for non-material aspects, like love, peace and calmness.

Meditation helps to reduce the intensity of the thoughts. It is not possible to generate full benefit from meditation without adopting good values that emphasis on love, honesty and simplicity. Both meditation and purity of thoughts work complementary to each other to bring calmness of mind. During meditation, mind is allowed to relax. With suitable modification in our attitude and practice, the intensity of thoughts gradually gets subdued. A stage during the practice may come when thoughts will come and move away without much trouble. With further practice, mind will imagine about divine essence, as it becomes aware that inner self is divine only. In the process of meditation, a feeling of lightness which is akin to love and peace will be felt.

Meditation is useful to reduce impulsive nature and bring focus in life. The distraction of mind is a disturbing trend which if continued unabated is harmful. People discuss about need to control distractions of mind; it is meditation that is a practical tool to move from lower level of distractions to higher level of absorption, filled with eternal peace, love and calmness. Attempt towards meditation is to attain these capabilities and search for reality which mere knowledge fails to provide. After meditation, we feel calm and relaxed.

CHAPTER FIFTY-FOUR

MORAL VALUES

Morality issues are essentially linked to understanding truth in life. At first sight, finding full meaning of life from inner consciousness becomes difficult. However, as people get absorbed in this thought, they find it to be reality. What you believe to be real turns to be temporary. Your material possessions, aspirations and successes are not all that you like to search in life. Inner consciousness is that spark which connects us with the Ultimate. It makes us to think about ultimate and what is that which we can carry from this life to other life and thereafter. It prompts to redefine every aspect of life in the broader perspective.

Everyone likes to be successful and comfortable in life. It may be possible to achieve success and fame without insisting on so called moral values like truth, honesty, simplicity and compassion. We find people successful and acquiring prosperity without being rigid on moral issues. They look for available opportunity to gain wealth and fame. This is the reason that morality is not treated as a dire necessity by so many people.

There has to be some compelling reason for reinforcing moral values. As we try to search for mystery of life and death, it provides a completely different perspective of life. This perspective of life is gained by knowing about our inner consciousness which is beyond body consciousness. Our inner consciousness remains also after death as death only takes over bodily consciousness. Many puzzles of this life gets resolved with this understanding that this life of ours is not an end itself, but we are here in this life and various lives thereafter and had been in existence in many more lives earlier. Our success, fame and wealth in this life are only a short and a temporary moment in the total cosmic existence. What we turn to be major purpose of life may not actually be any significant achievement when taking our existence in totality. With this awareness, people try to again look for the main purpose of existence. The spark that connects us with the Ultimate and its creation is Love. Our self in its true sense a spark of divine energy. The moment we lose this spark of energy consisting of love, we are dead.

Dealing with others with Love is not easy. Bodily consciousness always directs us to think of self. True Love demands surrender, sacrifice, gratitude, contentment, simplicity and other virtues. What we understand about love is actually being nice to someone. Divine Love has a much bigger connotation. Our soul or inner consciousness will feel fresh and renewed and close to Ultimate by being in divine love. It is nothing but deriving meaning of reality, it is divine love or love for divine, love for real essence that remains with us for this life and thereafter. It may appear to be too hypothetical at the first instant, but it is reality of our existence and a way towards spirituality. Moral values can thus be reinforced by considering the broader purpose of life, a life of being aware of inner consciousness.

The fear that holding on moral values will bring some sort of sacrifice and suffering makes most people to avoid sticking firmly to such values. These sufferings and discomforts from material front are too little compared to the benefit these provide in providing inner peace and purity of thought. It helps engaging mind in positive thinking. The perception about moral values may change from person to person but core moral values dependent on love, honesty, integrity, truthfulness and gratitude are not likely to be doubted.

DEBATING

In debate or discussion, we express our views based on the facts of the case and other person may present a contrary view. The purpose of the debate or a discussion is to help in taking reasoned decision based on all the facts of the case. However, it is often noticed that we lose calmness and these debates turnout to be heated conversations, thereby creating problem in relationship with others. At times, we are bogged down by emotions and prejudices while debating on the issue which evades facts. When we use emotions with no rational reasoning to sway people to our side of an argument, we are likely to be criticized by people that realize this as a tactic. It is crucial to control our emotions during these discussion and debate so as to restore peace of mind.

Staying calm during an argument is perhaps one of the most difficult challenges a person can face. Keeping composure when we feel passionate about something is easier said than done. Keep cool by using strategies to diffuse anger and tension, approaching the discussion with the right attitude, and relaxing body can help in maintaining calmness.

It's not easy to stay cool when things get heated in meetings, negotiations, or during difficult conversations. We might say something that we later regret, or get stuck on one point trying to prove that we are right, ultimately losing sight of the bigger picture. It may turn out that we have damaged trust in a broader relationship with a colleague, client, vendor, or spouse.

The fight-or-flight instinct that can arise in the course of a pointed discussion is largely an instant reaction. The mind attempts to rapidly process changing conditions and on becoming stunned by this, we perceive the situation as threatening. That is to say, emotional state becomes heightened as mind carefully prepares itself for the possibility of confronting a threat. The heart rate goes up, face turn red, and breathing becomes more shallow. As things get turned up, the risk is losing on rational thinking, and then it becomes difficult to be at our best self.

Rather than considering and planning for how someone else might attempt to defeat our argument, we may focus efforts on reinforcing potential weaknesses in reasoning. This allows to concurrently improve mental preparedness and construct a sound and valid argument.

Realize that the point of the meeting is not to prove who is right or wrong or who smartest person is. Rather, the purpose of debate or discussion is to resolve problem and find a joint solution. Let us not take things personally. It is better not to get impacted by conversation, rather let us be observer and take all the arguments in right spirit. We ought to develop capacity to listen other person carefully and appreciate his point of view. It will create healthy environment during discussion.

Let other person vent his feeling in an argument. By allowing the other person to vent, we also gain access to other important facts, assumptions, and constraints at play for bridging the gap with the other person. Rather than treating other person's concern as a criticism, you can bridge the gap and get on the same side of the conversation. If upon hearing the other person's viewpoint, we realize having made a mistake, then it is better to admit it rather than being defensive.

CHAPTER FIFTY-SIX

ADVICES

People try to offer advices to others without being asked. Someone have the habit of providing advices to colleagues, family members and other people. They do not know whether other person requires their advices. This habit often creates misunderstanding in relation. Nobody wishes to listen to other person unless he has trust on that person. People do not wish others to sit on judgment. Offer your suggestions but not advices. Be polite to express your views and respect the feelings of other person. Let us not think we are the only person to advice others.

Advising others make that person feel low and inferior. We may not be fully aware about the whole situation. The advice provided even with good intention and concern may not be ideal. Understand the situation fully and then try to help someone. Do not sit on judgment. Our spouse does not like to be offered advices. How we feel if someone comes with one or the other advices. If we are sympathetic towards other person, it has to reflect in our behaviour and attitude. Once other person reposes confidence and faith in us, he will look for our advices and suggestions. This is the moment when we may help the person through our advices and suggestions. Advising others have to come out of genuine feeling of love and concern for the other person. Before, we advise someone, examine whether we feel sympathetic and compassionate about other person. Is their genuine feeling to feel sympathy for the person? The first step is to listen, followed by being compassionate and only thereafter to offer advice.

People prefer to take advice from a person who is considered superior, knowledgeable, wise and compassionate. These advices ought to help other person. However, look for the main reason for offering some advices to the other person. Most of the time, it is our disagreement, compliant or superiority complex being reflected in the guise of advices. People understand the intention of these advices and feel bad.

It is desirable to first listen to the other person and feel sympathy for him. The act of listening is more effective and brings satisfaction to the person compared to offering advices. People feel connected during listening. Perhaps most people expect us to listen to them. Thereafter, find out whether they expect you to find way to deal with their problem. Make self-capable to offer any advice, before venturing to get into this habit. If you are suggesting something to the other person, be sure that you have good feeling about other person in offering such advices. When intention to offer advices are selfish, it rarely get acceptance from other person. It is better to avoid offending people with your advices.

Before advising others, please verify whether you are fully aware of the entire situation and whether it will genuinely help other person. In case you would have been in his/her situation, do you would have also followed similar advice? Are you able to help other person to carry out your advice? What are obstacles that can come in the way? Is your advice out of genuine concern for the other person or simply to show your knowledge and superiority over others? People in professional field also are in habit to advise others without fully evaluating the consequences. Similarly, senior member in the family advises others on various issues and expects them to follow these advices. Let us be discreet in giving advice and offer only when it is requested by others and will be helpful.

CHAPTER FIFTY-SEVEN

SPIRITUALITY

Spirituality describes about our real essence which is "spirit", "soul", "divine energy" or "inner consciousness". It deliberates on the connection this inner consciousness has with the Ultimate and how to realize and feel its essence. It tells us that our soul is representative of God. Everyone is spiritual in essence. We are just like son or daughter of God. All other people are our brothers and sisters. God is lying within us. His image or essence is lying within us. We have to recognize it by shedding outer layers filled with too much ego, greed and desires. Soul is connection with God.

As God is perceived to be lying somewhere else, may be at a far off place and not looking towards us all the time, we tend not to focus our attention towards HIM all the time. It is however difficult to develop a one to one relation with God when we perceive him to be staying somewhere at far off place, may be in heaven and is different from us. This imagination of

God staying in heaven creates space barrier which for an ordinary person is difficult to ignore. Spirituality tells that we are replica of God and his essence is lying within us. It is easy to form a close relation with someone who is inside us. Once we feel that presence of God is inside us; our breath is because he works within us; our heart beats because he is within us; then gradually this thought helps us to feel his presence at every instant. If we do something wrong, we realize that it is against our inner consciousness, therefore against God consciousness, and that our actions are viewed all the time.

The essence of spirituality lies in bringing God in the realm of own consciousness. This one to one relation brings faith to see HIM closely in our existence. This realization makes us to do all that which helps in becoming like HIM. God is seen as embodiment of virtue and to see and feel HIM, it expects us to adopt all those virtue to feel his essence. The spirit of spirituality can be experienced by going deep inside through regular practice, that helps in purifying our thoughts and realizing connect with other people through love and compassion.

The feeling of spirit helps in discarding some attributes like ego, greed, superiority complex and anger as they do not jell with it. These feelings come to a person who feels separate and in competition with other people. Spirituality talks of oneness despite outside dissimilarities. A person is not likely to develop superiority complex despite being expert in any field who realizes it does not matter in the broad spectrum of spiritual existence. Believing in spirituality widens horizon and every other person becomes our spiritual brother and sister and very close to us. These behavioural changes are beneficial for overall emotional well-being and happiness.

The notion of spirituality lies within us and it is not something alien. Spiritual experiences and Spirituality are not the privilege of a select few. With self-discipline and commitment, people can build foundation of spirituality. Spirituality does not talk about any doctrine, but expects to develop feeling within to remain attached to others and to HIM with love, and by shedding negative attitudes. Spiritual awareness makes a person to look into inner connectedness with other people that helps to get rid of many negative emotions popped by body consciousness. People, who remain attached to spirit in whatever manner, may be through meditation, prayer or remembrances develop faith in the usefulness of spirituality and generate long lasting peace.

CHAPTER FIFTY-EIGHT

HOPE

A person may face problems and difficulties, but hope makes difficult situations look simple. Hope visualizes future better than the present. The hope for better things makes us to work towards achievement of the desired goals. Hope is a big stimulant as it keeps a person charged with positive energy. People live with hope; once we lose hope, we are dead in our spirits and enthusiasm even when alive physically.

A person can remain in peace despite various adversaries by developing hope for the better things to come. Difference between happiness and otherwise is the attitude of hope. People derive hope in the fair judgment by God; a person who faces difficulty still hope to get fair treatment in later years. It is common to believe and hope that our troubles and difficulties will not live with us for ever, and with this hope our day to day setbacks do not trouble us.

Hope is derived from faith in God. Whenever, we face problems we believe that God will take care and protect us. This faith developed by people believing in religion and spirituality keeps them hopeful of contented and peaceful future. Hope is an outcome of positive energy flowing within, which directs us to face the challenges of life with courage. Thinking that our good deeds will not get waste creates hope, and onset of it brings peace and generates happiness.

The faith in the efficacy of our actions is a driving force with most people believing in Hindu philosophy. As per Hindu philosophy, doing good deed will be suitably rewarded either in this birth or subsequent birth. Similarly, a person's suffering may have to do with his past deeds. This philosophy has gone deep in the minds of most of the people believing in Hindu religion. It acts as a great guiding factor to face the difficulties in life as a result of our past actions, and promotes to do some good deed in an effort to be rewarded in subsequent birth. It makes people to adopt a righteous path of good deeds. If we think that all actions need to be rewarded in the same birth make us feel bad if good deeds are not rewarded properly. We find lot of discrimination in the natural justice, if we believe all actions and rewards to be accounted for in the same birth.

Hope boosts our energy and immune system, prompts us to remain active and deal with the events unfolding before us in an effective manner. A person who acts with Hope reinforces confidence also to others and pushes them to hard work. Hope is antidote to so many worries and challenges. Without hope, we will be lost and not able to work to full potential. It is thus important to be hopeful despite failures and challenges. There is no point to grudge about failures as it will dampen our energies. People regain Hope on looking to broader perspective of life based on selfless service to mankind.

The efforts put in the hope for better condition in future makes people to remain satisfied and happy in both pain and comforts. Hope for the better future drives us to work hard and to overcome difficulties; onset of positive working environment and cordial relation, both at work place and with family and relations. The life is perceived to be pleasant, despite difficulties coming in the way. This justifies problems and fortunes, and directs us to remain calm in both these extremes.

CHAPTER FIFTY-NINE

FAILURES

Highly successful people are the ones who have also failed at some time in the past and learnt and came out from such situations. We usually only learn about these individuals and their companies once they have made it big. We admire their success yet rarely witness the immense struggle they went through to get there. By not being aware to their failures, we are only left to compare ourselves to their achievements. This in turn can make it hard for us to validate the mistakes we make and problems we experience. We often question our abilities, not realizing that hardship is required in order to succeed.

This way of thinking has made the world afraid of failure. Even from a young age we have been taught that being wrong and making mistakes are bad. Our mind itself uses painful memories of the past to provoke negative emotions like fear and anxiety to stop us from making those same errors today.

The concept of staying positive has been misused, misconstrued, and abused by all of us. It has nothing to do with smiling and being happy with everything that happens to you. Positive thinking, rather, is used so that we can learn, grow, and evolve from what we experience in life. This does not mean failure. It simply means that if you are faced with a setback, understand it is not your final destination. It is a stepping-stone in your journey that is getting you to where you need to be. Once you have taken some time to tread it off, you can then begin accepting what happened. The initial emotion will eventually dissipate and you can then slowly return your focus back to the issue at hand. It is better not to react immediately to failure, but analyse the lessons we learn from such failures to deal the situation differently for future. It ought not to be taken as a disgrace.

Most people do anything to avoid realizing that mistake has happened and remain in denial. If we do this, then we risk failing miserably in future. We fail by learning from our setbacks and making the necessary adjustments until we succeed. As we get more competent to analyse failures by looking to various possible options, we see the positive side in even the toughest of situations.

When people hold a negative perception of themselves, it is not surprising that they feel quickly defeated when faced with challenges. It is important to know your strengths, when faced with challenges to boost your self-esteem. It is worth to realize that success and failures depend on so many factors, beyond your control. Rather than getting bogged with failures, take it as step forward for success. Hence, success and failure ought not to define you as a person, you are more than your accomplishments.

Relationship offer us support in both practical and emotional ways. They generally view you positively, even though they might have different opinions. By being open to their positive ways of perceiving you and their good feelings about you, you will cultivate self-esteem. Similarly, you may deal with the failures of your close friends and relationships, by understanding, listening and showing empathy. Besides, you may provide them options to deal with the situation based on your expertize. Hence, despite being faced with failures, one can still retain peace by valuing achievements and taking some time to introspect.

CHAPTER SIXTY

BLAME

Blame can harm us, both when we blame others and also when we blame ourselves. Even for people standing on the side-lines, blame can be scarring as they take sides or fear that they may be next to be blamed. It is often not the immediate effects that is damaging, but the longer-term effect of blaming is creating a fear-based society where power is used to blame and dominate rather than support and develop others.

If someone blames, we feel hurt, angry, victimized and unloved. We might believe that these feelings are caused by the way the other person treated us, but they are actually coming from our own self-abandonment. How we treat self, in the face of how others treat us, has far more impact on how others are treating us. It is also worth analysing whether the blame inflicted to us is based on certain fact, and does it require any adjustment in our activity or behaviour. Rather than being hurt and losing on self-esteem, we ought to take it an opportunity to introspect, bring modification in our role and to make appropriate adjustment to deal with the person in future.

Anyone who is blaming may not hear anything you say, so there is no point in talking. When your loved one hurts you, it is better to avoid the person at that time and come back after some time and then may be you can talk about it. If the situation does not change by that time, then you will have to continue to take loving care of yourself. The goal is to stay open to your own feelings, keeping your heart unspoilt, rather than to punish the other person. This is very different than withdrawal. When you withdraw, you are angry. You close your heart and punish the other person by withholding your love.

It is not worth taking the other person's behaviour seriously. Whatever you might have done that triggered their upset, you never deserve to be humiliated for it. The fact that they are blaming you is their issue, so it is important to make sure you are not taking their unloving behaviour personally.

We blame others assuming that people are bad, and that they fail through carelessness or other intent. Yet this is seldom true. Most people do their best and, although this is not always good enough to prevent failure, this does not mean the person is bad. When you assume others are good, well-intentioned and reliable, you will treat them that way and they will consequently act more that way. When everyone else is blaming some helpless person, there can be significant social pressure to join in and blame that person too, even if you do not really know what that person done wrong. You may pause and think rather than following the lead of others. Blaming others can have reciprocating impact. The other person will also look to your weakness and start blaming you.

Forgive rather than blame when the person has done something wrong, even if they have mistreated you, seek ways to forgive them. If you try to understand them rather going straight into attack, then you give them the opportunity to apologize and to make things right. If you understand that the person was not careless or deliberate in their mistake, or if you can see how there are other factors that contributed towards the situation, then again it is easier to forgive. This way you make self and others come out of the blame game.

KINDNESS

Kindness is selfless service to help someone or to cheer somebody. The purpose of kindness is to make other person happy and feel good by your kind words and deeds. These days everyone is busy of doing something for self. In the process, he makes others feel bad, stressed out and small. This is common approach pursued by so many to move ahead and compete with others. There are people who need help. Some need physical help, while other needs emotional help, and for someone it has to be monetary assistance.

Kindness is feeling of love and concern for others. It is a need of inner-self to be kind to others and it has to reflect in our attitude and dealings. As people recognize this inner need, they tend to be more kind to others. Kindness flows from inner-self (soul) and involves physical, mental, emotional and spiritual process. The act of kindness can be shown through physical help, control on impulsive mind, depicting good emotional feelings and by bringing inner-spiritual connection with the other person. It improves self-esteem.

People can be truly kind to others if they bring control on impulsive mind, tolerate others and speak nicely. The differences with other person spoils our health as we feel angry, dissociated and hurt when take these differences seriously. People who tolerate differences with other people are more likeable; they derive respect; able to communicate effectively and find better acceptance from other people. The first step towards kindness is to tolerate differences. It is not enough to be kind to a person who is better placed compared to us. Please not discriminate in being kind and considerate to others based on their status and position. The people who are junior to us feel better when treated properly.

There are lots of people who are quick to point out fault and criticize a person when the going is tough. You can be kind to a person if you understand the person, his pain, anxiety and concern, listen to him and boost his morale and courage. We have to take care while talking so that in any way we do not hurt other person. There will be number of occasions in life when we will differ with others. Let us not make these differences to override our behaviour and attitude against other person.

Kindness comes with love, care, compassion and tolerance. Love is an emotion through which we try to connect with the other person. Being in love with others is an activity that is to think good of others and create such environment to make others feel happy. We will not be kind to others, if we do not make self capable for it. As we understand our spiritual essence, it will bring us very close to other people through act of kindness, love and oneness; irrespective of external disparities in material possessions, capabilities and background.

Kindness is virtue of divine. If you wish to express love to someone, it has to be through kindness. It is difficult to move with the flow of life and fulfilling divine purpose by not to be kind. Kind does not mean weak. One has to be tough in his purpose, deeds and dedication but kind to others in better understanding, encouraging and putting them in a comfortable situation. You have to be tough outwardly but kind at heart. Be tough not to tolerate any mistakes, but soft in not damaging someone. Kindness is the greatest strength for a human kind. It helps feel better and remain in peace.

CREATIVITY

Creativity is doing something at professional level or in leisure time which includes imagination and invention. It leads to better performance and makes activity pleasant. Being creative in professional field brings respect and advantage to both self and other person. If we have leisure time, it may be spent in various activities. It is common to find that mind does not remain fully engaged and thoughts disturb us. Similarly, at professional level, the work may be repetitive and boring. We can avoid disturbances of mind by being creative. We tend to avoid repetitive and hard work which is actually much worse than any pain created from the actual work itself. The need is to make it motivating so that we are tagged to it, by being creative.

Let us begin to work on ideas that we are blessed with, otherwise they will become stagnant inside us and eventually lead to loss of opportunity to improvise our lives. It might seem right on the outside, but inside we will be feeling bad not getting those ideas converted into actual work. Creativity may not be perceived useful all the time, but still taking small steps for being creative brings interest in life.

As we become creative, we begin to access our thoughts, feelings and beliefs. When we take the time and energy to develop our own ideas, we learn to understand, trust and respect our inner self, in turn enabling us to better express ourselves. You may be surprised at the resources, thoughts and impulses that you discover as you start being creative. When we create, we may start to enjoy our work, even if it is not recognized, displayed or presented to the public. We learn to gain confidence from expressing our ideas, thoughts and performing creative work. This confidence carries over into decisions we make in other areas of life.

Creativity is fun, and doing anything that brings joy reduces stress levels and improves quality of life. Obstacles and challenges throughout life are inevitable. However, when we make creativity a habit, we continue to learn new, resourceful ways of solving problems in our work place and in life. Creativity provides an opportunity to have complete freedom to do whatever you want. When it comes to creating, particularly creating art, there are no rules. If there are any rules, you can go beyond to be creative. The freeing feeling that comes from creating something out of nothing is one of the greatest joys of creativity.

When engaging in something creative, we are growing. Whether we realize it or not, that is just part of the entire process. The more we create, the more we learn about self, and the more we learn, the more we grow. We are both body, mind and soul. Our bodies need healthy food and proper exercise. But our mind need proper care. By giving an outlet for creativity, we allow mind to remain engaged and freedom to grow and express.

Engaging in creative activity brings a sense of balance to our life. Idle mind acts like a devil, it creates number of negative scenarios, antidote of it is to be creative. People who are creative spent their idle time into creative activity, which helps to come out of stressful situations, It augurs well for our well-being and means to help others. As we set aside time for our pleasure and enjoyment, it helps relieve stress and built-up tension. The enjoyment we gain from it, promotes to learn how to create even more. Creativity brings a continual learning process that helps us to grow. It keeps us absorbed in the activity that brings joy and satisfaction.

ASSUMPTION

Life is a bundle of choices, it is up to each individual to decide what to pick and what to leave. The choice does not always lie between good and bad, but between good and best. Know what is important for your evolution and self-actualization to help make choices accordingly. Better prefer not to spend time in wasteful and purposeless activities. The choice determines our personality. If we try to do things that help in rewarding righteous path, the results will be rewarding. The real understanding lies in capability to choose a right path.

The need is to re-look and re-examine assumptions that guide course of life. Our common understanding will make us to believe that success, comforts, prestige and status lead to overall satisfaction. However, the reality may be quite different and assumptions have to be reoriented for activities that bring overall satisfaction.

Life is short, we may realize at the last stage having

missed vital part of it in pursuit of unwanted success. It may grasp on us having carried all these material baggage, but void inside if lacking in inner calmness. It is thus desired to work for such type of success, and make efforts to achieve it for the sake of bringing peace and calmness, the ultimate need of inner self. Let success be not merely for the sake of success, it is to aim for welfare and happiness of self along with all the people around us.

As we drive our self in pursuit of success and the moment we succeed in our life, it makes us satisfied and happy. It does not stop at this level but we look for more success. At each stage, we hanker for more of success till we become engrossed in it to such an extent that we lose the real purpose of success. Success ought to make you and all those people around you be satisfied and peaceful. But, success in most cases becomes its sole purpose. We become rich to be happy but our efforts continue to be richer at every stage till we lose the real purpose of wealth that ought to bring satisfaction and happiness to us and to other people around us. Hence, our assumption that success leads to peace and happiness may not always hold good. We have to understand the true meaning of success in pursuit of overall peace and happiness.

The overall satisfaction in life is restored by living a

balanced life, taking care of self and others and to work for both material comforts while at the same time developing feeling of love, empathy and care. Think of success in the broader context by understanding of necessities of life, feeling concern for the welfare of the other people and developing attitude to help others. The need is to look to your assumptions and keep on testing it and re-examine whether it needs any change so as to keep on the right tact. It should act as a mirror that tells us how we look.

There are different ways to do and to act in a particular situation. Let us find out which action of ours' helps us to lead a life full of virtues and imbibe in us finer qualities of love, compassion and tolerance. Certain choices may provide us momentarily benefit, but it may not provide a long lasting happiness. Engaging in self-gratification like excessive eating, gambling, drinking could provide happiness for that moment but may lead in deterioration in values of life and health. Righteous path takes time to generate rewards. The pursuit of peace lies in developing patience to move on a righteous path. The assumptions that we hold to bring long lasting satisfaction, as against momentarily pleasures.

CHAPTER SIXTY-FOUR

COMFORTS

Somehow many of us believe that comfort brings happiness and eventually peace of mind. This is a myth. Depending on anything which is external cannot bring long lasting peace and happiness. Peace and happiness has to arise from within.

If comfort was the way to happiness and peace then all those who acquire lavish houses and costly cars should always be happy and peaceful. Even if they get stress and anxiety, they should look to various material possessions for deriving comfort and eventual peace of mind. Using this logic, those who have little possession to derive comforts from life ought to feel depressed and worried. However, it does not happen in this manner. We all know this is not true. Comforts are no guarantee for deriving long lasting peace and happiness. Mind yearns for one comfort to another and never gets satisfied with these possessions. The desire for more of these comforts in itself creates stress and uneasiness. These comforts provide happiness and joy for a temporary period. The aim of the life is to move ahead with peace and happiness which comforts alone cannot provide. While we may not shun comforts, but it requires something elusive to draw attention for achieving calmness within. Happiness and peace are dependent on mental state which is internal. Only when our mental state is comfortable, we will get happiness and peace. No external or materialistic comforts alone can provide peace of mind. External comforts can only give comforts to our physical body not to our mental self. Most of the times, we forget this simple fact. People do not take enough care to control distractions of Mind, and our educational system, societies and Governments also ignore this fact.

Parents provide comforts to children with the hope that it can make the future of their children better. Those parents who think like that do not realize that the reason why they are doing well in life is because their mind was trained to deal with hardships and yet remain happy. Biggest mistake they are making now is depriving their children to go through the experience of facing physical discomforts and yet keep mental state happy. Their children grow up to believe only comforts bring happiness and peace. They chase physical comforts in life for happiness and peace.

As we acquire physical comforts, our mind gets diverted from mental stress and anxiety for short while. We focus on these new acquisition. As long as we focus on new acquisition, we feel good. Soon we get used to the newly acquired comfort; it is no more an object of novelty. There after mind goes back to its original nature of anxiety and stress. The cases of depression and mental illness are common is due to dependence on physical comforts and doing little to develop intangible values. These come from developing positive attitude towards life. It includes courage, love, sympathy, compassion, friendship and hard work. Devoting time to bring these intangibles in the realm of our life diverts mind from comforts and discomforts. There is nothing wrong in availing various facilities to bring comforts in life. It makes life easy, provided mind does not hanker for more comforts that may not be easily available. This require modification in our attitude and behaviour as not to lay much emphasize on these comforts and enjoy them without getting too much bogged. In this manner, these comfort do not produce any negative impact and we remain at peace.

CHAPTER SIXTY-FIVE

COMPROMISE

To achieve peace and calmness in life, it requires avoiding conflicts, arguments and bickering. It will be difficult to maintain peace, if faced with stressful environment. It is not easy to isolate from conflicts completely while dealing with others. There cannot be any straight answer to all the problems. One of the ways to ease the tension is to compromise a bit from your stand so that other person cooperates and environment becomes conducive to work together. This does not however mean that we should compromise on our core values of honesty and integrity.

The problem with human behaviour is that we remain rigid on our stand while dealing with others. Most time our stand on certain issue is based on ego, emotions and prejudice. It becomes matter of ego, if we yield a bit from our stand. The other person often may take contrary stand. The first problem with fights is that everyone involved wishes to be right. We all want to win. It is understandable that we feel that way, but it is something we need to stop feeling. When we want to win, we are not listening to the other side of the argument or conversation. Needing to be right is just the first thing we need to avoid. This is true while dealing with colleagues, friends and family members. Lot of stress will go away, if we remind continuously that we will not be right all the time and agree and compromise with others.

Sometimes, we argue on a particular issue to prove that we are right. However, in the process connect with the other person is lost to understand his viewpoint. There are no straight right or wrong answers to an issue. These are all views and we should learn to respect divergent views. One way to avoid this is to stay calm when a discussion arises so you are not pulled into a fight. Keep emotions in check and think about what you really want, both from your life and from the relationship. Is it important to stand your ground so firmly, or would everything still be acceptable if to accommodate others' view point. This is important in all relationships, be it with our kids, siblings, partner or co-workers. It thus makes logic to be flexible and compromise on our stand for the good of own and other person.

It is one thing to say you are willing to compromise,

but entirely another thing to adhere on that change. If our expectations from other person is high and these are not being realized, the option available is to resent, fight, argue or compromise. Introspect and decide whether holding on our expectation is impacting adversely the relation and calmness. It needs our resolve to adopt compromise as way out to come out of the stressful situation. A major part of compromising is actually following through with the resolution. This will show others that you are willing to compromise completely, not just make false promises in order to end a fight. It is likely that other person will also yield from his stand and cordial relationship develops.

Compromise is one of the option to deal with the problem and ought not to be taken in a negative sense. It means being flexible while dealing with others. Being willing to compromise, instead of fighting until the finish, is an admirable trait. You show how much you appreciate the other person working with you to find the best solution. Take time to evaluate the solution together and express what you like about it. It is worth examining how we feel being appreciative of the positive interaction and working together to find the best solution. By doing so, we will be able to bring peace while dealings with others.

CHAPTER SIXTY-SIX

CALMNESS

Calmness can exist in the midst of stress, conflict, and vigorous action. Two people can have an intense verbal debate, yet it is possible even at such a time to be fully engaged but inwardly calm. Often in our lives peace eludes us. That is the time to concentrate on calmness. Let us refuse to become agitated by outer circumstances, and even in the midst of agitating events, remain calm inside. By cultivating calmness when it is easier, as during meditation, we can gradually develop the ability to remain peaceful in every circumstance. This is how Paramhansa Yogananda (Hindu Monk) described the progress of a devotee– at first, able to be calm only rarely, then calm some of the time, then calm all the time.

The calmness can exist even in the absence of peace. Once we notice self-criticism and judge at that moment, we have a chance to practice self-compassion. This means acknowledging and accepting reality, and extending the same kind of compassion to ourselves that we would to a good friend in that situation. In doing this, we stop comparing ourselves to other people. We may not be able to resist negative self-talk but can distance from it. Setting routine may become boredom, but at the same time it helps in day-to-day engagement that brings peace in our minds. When we have set routines, we have less decisions to make during the day. This frees up space in our minds for bigger, more important tasks.

There is no pattern to achieve calmness as everyone is different. What helps one person find peace and calm might have the opposite effect on the other person. Let us examine our thoughts and find if these are devoid of calmness. It is likely that we may be able to fix these distractions and move with confidence to face it. Nothing remains permanently with us. Any issue which troubles us will go away. Think, how many time in past we were worried and how these issues were resolved. Bringing realistic approach about any situation can reduce emotional turmoil and restore peace of mind.

As we go about our daily routine, notice when we feel most at ease and make note of what we were doing at that time. Some people feel calm while engaging in creative activity, while for others relaxing and listening to music provides momentarily calmness. Hence explore and create own list of activities that help mind to relax.

It is easy to get caught up in own stories, and to look for what is not going right in our lives. In fact, most people live this way. Most people also live with constant stress, worry or anxiety. If we want to remain calm, even in the midst of a crisis, focus on what is going right in our life and have to be grateful. It is not a big issue to remain calm when the external environment is conducive. One has to learn to remain calm at times when faced with tough challenges. Constant practice can bring resilience to face it.

Calmness can be restored, if we overcome fears and worries. These worries are mainly on account of threat of losing material comforts, recognition and success. The more we think of self, the chances are that it will lead us to stress and anxiety. Our needs undergoes change and no comfort can give a permanent calmness. Un-controlled negative emotions disturbs the mind. Hence, the only way to achieve peace and calmness is to divert from thinking of self and engage in activities for common good.

WEAKNESS

All of us have to realize that we are good at some things, just average at others, and bad at some. This can be frustrating because we want to be good at everything. We may believe to be good at everything, because of holding control of the corporate and responsible for its success. It is better to accept weakness gracefully in front of others so that they understand us better and do not make a fun of it. This will make us not to hide any thing and not burden with hiding facts from others. It is better to seek clarifications rather that presuming that we have understood everything. Further, it is not practical to overcome all weakness as the rewards may not justify the efforts.

If we think too much about weakness, it can create stress. One has to realize that these weakness are not unique to me, but prevails in one or the other way to all of us. Hence, let us not over-emphasize it but take necessary steps through planning and support from others to minimize its impact. Simultaneously, to avoid to make fun of other person by emphasizing his/her weakness. It is all the more important to help the person to overcome these weakness. Weakness can be of different type. Someone may not be able to perform any task properly, weak in analysis, not good in marketing, problems with effective communication, lacks adequate knowledge on particular issue and may be not good in inter-personal relations. However, it is not difficult to compensate these weakness.

You cannot turn a weakness into a strength, if busy denying that weakness exists. So first task is to recognize it and determine your weakness. Sometimes the best recourse against a weakness is to compensate with superb preparation. Alternatively, one can seek help from others to make good the weakness.

One thing that is often not so obvious is that our strengths can also be the source of our weaknesses. Every virtue can be misused or distorted. Being aware of strength can lead into stubbornness and unyielding behaviour in dealing with others. Hence, we lose chance to accept things as they unfold before us. When we are bogged down with strength and not able to accept views of others, we live in a world of isolation, low motivation, and weak will power. On the other end, we may use our strength to develop courage, boldness and will power to take action, and making an effort to change the situation to mutual benefit of all. Hence, both weakness and strength need to be understood and properly reinforced in our decision making while dealing with other people.

We may not be able to overcome our weakness in a particular area, and it may be a major reason for stress and anxiety. The best way is to deal with the particular weakness is to avoid such situation and to compensate it by way of other strengths. People will respect us for our strengths, provided we do not make a big issue of our weakness. Also, once we are aware of our weakness in any particular field, it is possible to seek necessary support from someone to move ahead. Whether it is in our work place or in family life, we ought to be sincere to discuss to compensate in areas where we are not fully updated. It does not matter if we are required to learn and listen on these issues from juniors. By doing so, they will feel committed and it will built cordial environment, reduce stress and impart peace and satisfaction.

CHAPTER SIXTY-EIGHT

EMPATHY

Empathy is the ability to understand and share the feelings of another person. To feel and display empathy, it is not necessary to share the same experiences or circumstances as others. Rather, empathy is an attempt to better understand the other person by getting to know their perspective. Psychologists Daniel Goleman and Paul Ekman break down the concept of empathy into the following three categories.

Cognitive empathy is the ability to understand how a person feels and what they might be thinking. So, before we engage with another person, consider what we know about them, and be willing to learn more. It makes us better communicators, because it helps us convey information in a way that best reaches the other person. Our interpretation of another person's mood, behaviour, or thinking are influenced by our prior experience and unconscious bias. Hence, our instincts may be wrong and it is imperative not to be quick to assume or rush to judgment.

Emotional empathy is the ability to share the feelings of another person. This type of empathy helps to build emotional connections with others. When a person tells you about a personal struggle, listen carefully. Resist the urge to judge the person or situation, to interrupt and share your personal experience, or to propose a solution. Instead, focus on understanding the how and why they feel that way. Once you have a better understanding of how the person feels, you must find a way to relate.

Compassionate empathy goes beyond simply understanding others and sharing their feelings. It actually moves us to take action and provide help in whatever manner we can. It is fine to share your experience or make suggestions, but avoid conveying the impression that you have seen it all or have all the answers. Provide the option that can be adapted to suit their requirement, and to avoid suggesting all inclusive solution.

Being emphatic has got several advantage, the most predominant one is on creating a healthy work environment. Empathy makes the office a happier place to be, where each person works not because they have to but because they want to. One of the best thing to reduce stress and improve health is to develop empathy. Compassionate people are better equipped to handle stress than their non-empathetic peers. Relief from stress is one of the many reasons everyone should bring empathy into the workplace. Teams who show respect and concern for one another are more likely to trust and value the input of everyone involved. In addition, team members who might not otherwise feel comfortable speaking up will feel like their voices are both valued and understood. And when challenges arise, they will be able to recognize each team member's point-of-view and find a solution faster.

These days personal life is borne with disliking, anger and disenchantment. Communication fails and stress grows both at work place and with family members. It is cause of worry and unhappiness. Under these circumstances, being empathetic, requires better communication and understanding that can work to improve work and family environment. Besides, it helps in achieving higher purpose of life to be loving and useful to others. Whether it is at office or at home, being empathetic creates peaceful environment.

CHAPTER SIXTY-NINE

ARGUMENT

Arguing is to speak for or against a proposal. Thus the arguments are considered necessary when we do not agree to a particular thing. If we do not argue, then it is presumed that we agree to the proposal. Arguments ought to be constructive and based on facts. We should be able to convince other person about our point of view and how it is for mutual benefit. While arguing, it is desirable not to bring emotions and prejudices to influence other person. It is difficult to remain cool and composed during argument, however one has to realize the overall importance and benefit of poise and calmness while arguing.

A common cause of frustration, anger and disappointment is that we cannot control emotions while arguing with other persons, and the more intimate they are, the more emotional we find ourselves. Because arguments can escalate due to mishaps in communication, it is important to take the necessary measures to stop, think, re-evaluate, and calm self before you say or do something you might regret. Anticipate when things go bad in an argument.

Being mindful of our voice, tone and surroundings help to keep emotions at bay and make us better able to communicate in a thoughtful manner. If we get angry, it might be best to get some fresh air, take a break, or sit in a different room alone for some time, depending on level of frustration. Furthermore, research has shown that breathing exercises can lower blood pressure and stress. Not only can taking a few deep breaths act as a much-needed pause to break the tension, but also it can bring back clarity in the mind.

In the middle of arguing over who takes out the abuse more, a part of brain activates, causing body to step into 'flight" mode. In this manner, heart beat accelerates as compared to people who do not argue as often.

Intense anger can trigger rapid breathing, which can sometimes make chest feel like it is contracting. However, deep breathing can trigger the opposite of the flight-or-fight response, slowing down all the horrible effects stress can cause on our system. A little bit of stress can actually boost immune system and help to impart responsibility in discharge of various functions, but too much stress over a long period of time can lead to declines in the function of immune system.

The important thing to remember in the heat of the moment is to keep calm. To reduce the ill impact of arguing, let us realize that it is not about winning or losing. It is not always possible to make another person to agree to our point of view. Maintain a neutral stand while arguing. Do not let other person feel low. Never show superiority complex. Let us be flexible to other options for the benefit of arriving at a solution. The need is to respect other person and his views while listening him carefully before we argue. Sometimes, because of ego, we tend to become rigid and do not yield while arguing. Even if we realize that the issue is trivial, but still we insist on our point of view. People have lost patience to listen to others and jump into arguing. Practicing positive communication behaviour like active listening and validating other person's feelings can curtail the stress and can bring calmness while arguing.

RESPECT

Respect means that you accept somebody even when they are different from you or you do not agree with them. Respect in your relationships generate feelings of trust and comfort. Receiving respect from others is important because it helps us to feel safe and to communicate with ease. Learning how to show respect to both your peers and those in positions of authority can change the course of our life. Noticing how in turn get respect from others can make journey of life easier.

All our work proceeds effectively and successfully when we work in an environment of respect for others. Offering Respect requires a conscious decision and deliberate action. It is expressed both overtly and tacitly. It is not words, but behaviour that reflects true respect for others. Showing respect is the only way to make it reciprocated. Calm in the face of anxiety or provocation is among the most powerful peaceful messages we can send. To be calm is to trust and respect others.

You want to be respected, but you are not sure how this whole thing works. The key here is to stop focusing on you, and start thinking about others. Think how you can inspire change for growth to others. Take initiative and use skill and resources to start getting things done and solve problems. Always honour commitments and promises. If you find yourself having a lot of trouble with that, it means you make too many promises you cannot keep. People who are constantly saying, "I am sorry," without giving it a second thought are usually not the ones that are well respected. There is a time and place for apologies.

If you respect others' time, they will respect yours. This includes not being late for appointments, not talking about trivial items during meetings, getting to the point fast, bringing up issues right away, being brief, and making it easier for others to make decisions. If you criticise others in their absence, your reputation will be impacted. Let us understand that we are not going to be right, and not the best at everything. Every person you meet can teach you something. Confidence does not come from a place where you are the best. True confidence comes from understanding humility.

We will be respected by finding ways to offer valuable suggestions to others. It can come in many forms, but in the end, it is offering something that can help by solving a problem for others. You can be inspiring by encouraging others to follow their dreams, goals, visions, and showing that you have faith in them. Let us not feel guilty about saying no once in a while. Do not worry about missed opportunities. Let us hold on to creativity and follow through with our ideas. It is utmost important to curb instant reactions to things that make us highly emotional, thereby finding it difficult to understand and respect others. It is better to know as when to respond and when to react. It is better to be discreet in reacting as it is not a good habit. Start caring others, whether it is at work, home or neighbourhood.

The cardinal principle is to listen, care and be polite to others to be respectful. Still, if somebody does not respect, we should learn to be respectful to him for our own good. As we pay attention to these attributes, it will in turn create respect for us and bring peace and calmness.

CHAPTER SEVENTY-ONE

PROMISE

Promise is to tell someone to undertake something in future. It is assurance given to others that you will meet their requirement as promised in future. This assurance by way of promise brings comfort to others. They move ahead and plan for future based on these promises. However, it is important that the promise made are obeyed. People are generally found to make promise but are not committed to obey it. By making promises in this manner, they try to derive some benefit from others, knowing very well that they are either not in a position or not willing to recognise it at a future date. This attitude in the long run can impact trust from others. We have to be careful while making promise to others that we are capable to keep it and these are meant to be fulfilled. By not keeping promise, we have to hide the real reason and tell lies and in the long run it creates environment of miss-trust. One of the most important characteristic to keep promise is to avoid thinking self-interest all the time, but to work for mutual welfare of others.

Let us pause for a moment and find why we are making Promises to others. Do we want to be seen as man of virtue in front of others or there is genuine feeling to help and obey the Promises. We will have to curtail the habit of not keeping the promises and examine the consequences it has on the other person. As we become conscious of this habit and make self accountable to keep promise, it will bring discipline and commitment in life. Avoid lose talk and be specific while making commitment. Sometimes, to gain immediate support from others, we tend to make a false promise knowing fully well that it will not be obeyed. Let us be sensitive that other person based on our promise, moves ahead and carries certain activities and likely to suffer if we fail to fulfil our promises. This attitude if becomes habit, creates situation of mistrust. With regard to financial matters, if we promise someone help to take care of his exigencies, let us be sure that these promises and commitments will be made on time. With this behaviour, we gain credibility and respect from others. The dealing remains cordial and calm.

We enter into contracts with others, still if situation is not favourable, tend to find ways to come out of it and break these promises. We take recourse to various lacunae in legal documents to come out of our commitments. While, it may be permissible legally, but may not be morally right. Hence, while breaking promises made to others, let us think and pause whether we are moving away from adhering to higher values of life.

Most of us are in the habit of saying "Yes" to our colleagues and family members; knowing very well that it may be difficult to agree to their suggestion. You do not want to annoy your colleague or family member by saying "No". In this manner, it creates lot of stress as you are fully aware that his/ her request is not acceptable to you. Let us avoid such situation and gain strength to say "No" when warranted. Doing this way will reduce stress level. We also make promise to self and find it difficult to keep it. As we break own promises, it impacts self-confidence. Be specific and be sincere about what you are promising yourself, and are you serious to adhere to do. Keeping promises is a way to enforce discipline in life. Promises is a way of planning our life and commitments. It gives opportunity to look for what we need to do in future for self and others. It is a way to express our need to connect with others. The cardinal principle to achieve peace is to make promises that we are able to obey, to make all efforts to accomplish these promises so that not to create harm to others.

CHAPTER SEVENTY-TWO

FRIENDSHIP

Friendship for most people is a combination of affection, loyalty, love, respect, and trust. True friendship is when someone knows you better than yourself and takes a position in your best interests in a crisis. Friendship goes beyond just sharing time together, and it is long lasting.

We all live in a society and understand how important friends are for us. We have got friends with whom shop, have lunch, spend leisure time, discuss and seek help. Having a best friend is a good thing, it makes our life more complete, exciting and fun. You feel comfortable when your friend is around. This person creates your comfort zone, and spending quality time with him/her helps decrease stress levels. Having a close friend around can lift our mood very quickly. Besides, it means that every time our friend makes us smile, he/she makes our thoughts more positive and makes us a happier person. The person knows you best, remains aware about your strengths and weaknesses and can provide you constructive feedback of these qualities, and helps to overcome limitations. Having a real friend to share things that helps to learn new things about yourself. A best friend is always ready to share not only your good times but also help you in tough times.

In most cases, friendship brings comforts and channelizes energy in positive manner. Friendship is developed with people having similar attitude and likes. The purpose of life is to move ahead in peace and happiness. This can be achieved through love, affection, trust, humility and sincerity. One has to thus ponder whether friendship with someone adds to these values. Is your friend, helping to create a better environment? Is your friendship more oriented to enjoyment? Do you keep lot of expectation from your friend? What if they are not satisfied? Is friendship developed for deriving benefit? As we ponder on all these aspects, it helps us to conceptualize true value of friendship with others.

Friendship in certain cases can turn to be damaging. Whether your friendship is leading to compromise your core values. Is it pushing you to activities that drain your energy? It becomes difficult to resist such tendency when you are in the company of close friends. One has to self-examine to avoid any long term adverse impact. Friend for the sake of friendship does not help. The relationship ought to be compatible and add to your strength, more during difficult situations. Let us examine whether the friendship is not creating any hindrance in enjoying life with peace and calmness.

One need to have sufficient time for own self. If one has got lot of friends, it requires too much socialization and spending time in activities that may not be useful. Hence, need is to be discreet in developing Friendship. The time for remaining in solitude is to remain attached to inner self and to reduce outer chatting. This is a way to gain calmness. Hence, keep track of activities that need to be carried with your friends to keep both of you in good humour and help in boosting emotions.

In Friendship, it is opportunity to show love and compassion. It takes us away from selfish tendencies and prompts to think of common good of others. Let us not keep expectations from others and develop friendship on the basis of mutual respect and care. As we develop these attributes, it creates a positive feeling within us. In this way, small irritants does not affect.

CHAPTER SEVENTY-THREE

LEISURE

Leisure has often been defined as free time spent in non-compulsory activities. Free time is time spent away from business, work, job hunting, domestic chores, education, as well as any other necessary activities. People look for free time so that they can spend it in the activities they cherish most.

Nowadays, we are extremely busy in attending to jobs and family. It requires working for long hours. Time does not stretch long enough to enable us to do everything. At one point of fast-paced life, body will manifest its tiredness. Either through physical exhaustion, stress, mood swings, anger, or laziness that body will provide enough signal, it will alert that we need to make some changes in lifestyle. Most times, small changes will be enough to see improvements.

During leisure, we are free from compulsory physical activities, but mind may still continue to be disturbed.

Hence the activities we choose during leisure time ought to take care of both physical and mental rest and pleasure. Dealing with emotions and overcoming negative thoughts is the most important activity during leisure time. On the contrary, people during leisure time do not know what to do and spend time in brooding over the past or worries about future. They recollect hurt inflicted by others and develop self-pity. Hence, leisure does not give any mental comfort when we engage mind with these negative talk. People thus find it more convenient to be engaged in work than leisure.

We know that there are things that go beyond our control, but there are others that we can control. We find it easier to manage time and tasks, when remain less stressed and more positive with life. A sedentary lifestyle puts us at risk for serious diseases and also for emotional distress. By engaging in physical activities during leisure time, we can improve physical and consequently mental health. Choosing recreational activities does not have to be an extensive plan. Be spontaneous and follow as per your needs and moods. One day you may choose a long walk on the park, the next time it could be to listen to music, another time for social activity. The purpose is to keep mind feel light and relaxed. These activities can be different for each individual depending on particular choice. By plunging into tasks without having a break, the productivity decreases. We become slower, mistakes will appear. This affects negatively productivity. Stepping away from work and making time for leisure clears mind and nourish problem-solving skills. When overloaded with work, it is when we need leisure time.

Leisure is fundamental to balance working life with personal development: it allows to stop, and to connect with self. Remember, leisure is a time to connect with own self and with others including family members. More often, we are not able to enjoy leisure time with others due to negative emotions. Let us not bring differences in human relations to spoil leisure time. It is an opportunity to introspect and looking for purpose of life. Leisure time helps to think what we should aspire in life. It is time to engage in those activities that give peace and pleasure. One has to be discreet in utilizing leisure time. The purpose of leisure time is to engage in activities to improve the mood and get rid of negative emotions. The purpose is defeated, if not able to get rid of these anxieties during leisure time.

DIET

The human body requires essential nutrients on a daily basis to function properly. We know from medical research that a lack of these nutrients can cause chemical imbalance in organ and brain functions. Ancient practitioners of Ayurvedic medicine — the world's oldest surviving healing system — created a lifestyle in which the body and mind maintain optimal health and mental well-being. The practice of Ayurveda distinguishes food as having particular energetic qualities, known as *sattvic* (lightness, purity), *rajasic* (overactive, passionate), and *tamasic* (lethargy, inertia). These energies are universal in dimension and permeate all living and inanimate life. Eating too much of rajasic or tamasic foods will create a chemical imbalance in the brain. Instead, it is suggested to eat these foods in moderation and aim for living a sattvic lifestyle.

The *sattvic* diet is considered the purest, the most

suitable for anyone, but especially for the people who look for spiritual attainment. It nourishes the body and creates a peaceful and calm state of mind. A sattvic diet leads one to attain optimal health, a peaceful and focused mind, with a balanced flow of energy. Sattvic foods include fresh and dried fruit and vegetables, whole grain cereals and breads, fresh fruit and vegetable juices, raw milk, butter and cheese, legumes, nuts, seeds, honey, fresh herbs and herbal teas etc.

A *tamasic* diet causes energy to decline, depresses the mind, and causes the person to become dull, lazy and unmotivated. The body's immune system is weakened and the mind filled with emotions like anger and greed. These foods include non-vegetarian items like meat, fish, chicken, eggs; alcohol, tobacco, drugs, fermented foods, such as vinegar fried foods, mushrooms and stale or overripe foods.

Rajasic foods over-stimulate the brain causing anxiety, stress and nervous disorders. Rajasic foods are very hot, bitter, sour, dry or salty. Too much rajasic food or eating too fast will over-stimulate the body and excite the passions, making the mind restless and uncontrollable. Rajasic foods include hot peppers, garlic and onions, coffee and caffeinated tea, refined sugar, soft drinks, chocolate, over-salted foods etc.

Thus while taking any food, it is to be kept in mind that it attains our overall needs. These include giving enough strength to the body as also to keeping our mental faculties in tune with our aspirations. If we hanker for peace and calmness, we have to choose the food that contributes towards attaining it.

People all around the world are now realizing benefits of a vegetarian diet. The reasons range from health and economics to ethics and religion. The physiological comparisons indicate that the human body is designed for a vegetarian diet. Besides, many religious faiths across world advocate vegetarian diet as killing animals is considered cruel. As we believe in God and develop love and compassion for his creations, it normally emanates to us to avoid non -vegetarian diet. Taking clue from various religious texts, proper selection of diet helps in developing inner condition that is conducive to spiritual growth. These texts emphasis on vegetarian diet. Let us develop a taste for simple vegetarian diet so as not being instrumental in inflicting cruelty on animals for our own peace of mind.

CHAPTER SEVENTY-FIVE

GUILT

Guilt is a feeling people typically have after doing something wrong, intentionally or accidentally. A person's sense of guilt usually relates to their moral values. It is not necessarily bad all the time. It can be productive when after making a mistake can lead to transformation, such as an apology or a decision to make different choices in the future. But guilt is sometimes obstructive. It can cause physical symptoms, self-doubt, decreased self-esteem, and shame. It can be difficult to overcome these feelings, especially in the case of chronic guilt. Hence, the nature consequence of this feeling is to repent on these actions and feel unhappy. People curse self for these feelings of guilt. It can be a vague and hard-to-predict when it impacts us. Some feel it much stronger than others. Feelings of guilt are quite common among those with mental illnesses like anxiety and depression.

When guilty feelings compete for your attention with

the demands of work and personal life, guilt usually wins. The concentration, productivity and creativity remain significantly lower when guilt occupies mind. Even mild guilt can make difficult to embrace the joys of life. But for some people, guilt can do even worse damage. Even though you might have already caused someone harm, you may make matters worse by distancing yourself from that person. You end up feeling guilty about impacting others adversely, when you actually have not. Hence, guilt feelings expose us to constant and unnecessary stress and impacting own quality of life. It is a "burden" in more than one way.

Guilt happens when a person believes they have acted against either their own personal beliefs of what is morally good or the standards society has for acceptable behaviour. The guilt is also the result of thinking about acting against personal moral standards or the standards of society. When a culture or religion holds that a certain behaviour is wrong, a person may feel guilty even if their own moral code tells them there is nothing wrong with the behaviour.

Feeling guilty often stems from an underlying sense of responsibility towards other people. It could also arise from unresolved problems, strained emotions and personal feelings of unworthiness. It can arise from refusal to accept your mistakes. No matter what the reason is for your guilt, you are feeling guilty for a reason, and it reminds of heading in the wrong direction. Hence, the choice is to reconsider to take a different path moving forward. In fact, let us see guilt as an opportunity to re-examine and correct our behaviour. It is an opportunity to correct the wrong and move ahead in life in a more positive way. Instead, you must take responsibility for your mistakes. It is time to imagine new possibilities. It will serve no good to brood on guilt but to take responsibility to rectify the wrongs done. We can still do certain things to help improve circumstances and eliminate feelings of guilt.

To avoid feeling of guilt, let us not over-commit or over-promise as it may arise feeling guilty, when not able to deliver on your promises. Do not indulge in self-blame and avoid to associate with people who blame and unreasonably criticize. Do not live with impractical expectations or standards. You will end up feeling guilty because you simply cannot live up to the standards. As we refine attitude and behaviour, it may reduce guilt feelings. This will help to enjoy our journey while keeping focus on acquiring peace and satisfaction in life.

CHAPTER SEVENTY-SIX

DONATION

One of the major positive effects of donating money to charity is feeling good about 'giving'. Being able to give to those in need provides personal satisfaction. It generates positive feeling on helping others. At the core of our existence is the feeling of oneness with other people. As we dwell on the bigger picture, it becomes clear that all people have come from same source. Thinking about it, a feeling of love and compassion develops towards others; and inner-consciousness craves for helping others. This is the major reason why people donate to others who are in need of such help. Instead of putting money toward a gift someone may look at once and never use again, you may donate that money to a charity in need on behalf of your family members. This creates a feeling of self-worth by realizing that we are offering much-needed resources for a great cause for those in need. As an added benefit, you and your family members feel good about giving back to others.

Studies show that donating money to charity has been proven to have a positive impact. These effects are similar to activities people usually associate that provide joy and happiness such as eating, exercising or affectionate gestures like giving someone a hug. There are many advantages of helping others, as donating can help to fulfil urgent needs of the other person. A donation is a gift for charity, humanitarian aid, or to benefit a cause. A donation may take various forms, including money, alms, services, or goods such as clothing, toys, food, or vehicles. A donation may satisfy medical needs such as blood or organs for transplant.

It is no surprise that stress, depression and anxiety can create health issues. One of the reason why donating is good is that it acts as a way to de-stress our life. With the simple act of charitable giving, we perceive to receive the blessings from other person. The higher purpose of life is to connect with other people through love, sincerity and empathy. The best way to serve this purpose is to contribute through donation. Depending on the capability, donation can be either in monetary or non- monetary basis.

The gift of giving always comes full circle. In some way, the moment we are engaged in helping others through donation, nature also makes us eligible to receive the help when we are in need of the same in the manner it best suits us. The moment we think about our peace and overall satisfaction in life, consider positive benefits that donating can bring about and positive change it can bring around us. We believe every child around the world deserves a bright future. Making a donation to charitable organizations that work for child welfare who need it most is for a noble cause. However, one must be discreet in donating for a good cause and ensure the same reaches to the needy person and not wasted in between. This requires necessary verification of the credentials of the organizations to whom you would like to donate.

Whether we offer emotional support for loved ones, volunteer time to assist an organization, or donate money to charity, these means of donation enhances self-esteem and health benefits. To develop practice of donation require to keep a portion of earnings to be donated. It generates positive feeling that we have contributed back to the society. As we achieve success and wealth, we feel grateful to God and society. One way to pay back to the society is to donate. It is a divine trait and way to connect with other people.

CHAPTER SEVENTY-SEVEN

ALOOF

Aloof person is someone who is not friendly, instead being distant and reserved. That person generally keeps to self and does not prefer to spend time in conversation with others. When we think of an aloof person, we deem that person as uninterested, detached, and a little cold. Despite these negative connotation, aloofness can actually be useful sometimes. May be you need to shut out difficult people in your life. Whatever be the reason, you first need to understand when it is appropriate to be aloof, and when it is not. Then, you can work on being aloof by limiting conversation, appearing busy, and staying cool. If you see people conversing in a group, do not approach them. If someone tries to strike up a conversation, respond politely, but keep the conversation brief. Tell the other person it was nice talking to them to wrap things up. Being aloof is all about seeming disinterested, so do not get into detailed conversation. Even in tense situations, let us remain cool and calm.

Hence, aloofness in certain situation can help to remain in peace but it is not ideal in all situations. Thus there is nothing good or bad about being aloof. It depends on the situation. Sometimes, to avoid messy situation in conversation with others, it may be better to be aloof. If you are not feeling emotionally attached to someone due to past behaviour, aloofness can be helpful. At other time, it may be useful to come out of your shell and open up your feelings. That way it can bring relaxation. Hence, one has to understand the value of developing close bonding with others.

When it comes to being cool and distant, it is a way to avoid the perceived or real experience of rejection. Possible causes to such behaviour could result from being ignored or rejected. A way to relieve these painful memories, we use aloofness to cope with the situation. If we look for something, be it love or acceptance from other person and it is rarely there, we then begin to withdraw and hold back as a way to protect ourselves. There is also our interpretation of behaviour that can cause us to withdraw from other person and prefer remaining aloof. There might be other factors involved, the person is shy, quite or that there is currently something going on in their life that is causing the aloof behaviour. The person may not be interested to contribute to the conversation.

The same situation may be applicable to other person who prefers to dissociate with us and remain aloof. Our close relation, family member and friends may prefer to remain aloof from us. The past experience dealing with us might not be good for them. We might have ignored or rejected them. To regain peace and bring warmth in the relation, it is preferable to be sensitive to the feelings of others. Let our action and behaviour not drive someone to aloofness. We need to develop a special rapport with people close to us who remain aloof. Examine whether our behaviour keeps them aloof from us.

It may be difficult to know specifically what causes a person to distance themselves. They may not want you to know, and that is fine. But have empathy when reaching out. The person may be struggling to share his feelings. He may be embarrassed or scared of being vulnerable. Hence, we can reveal part of our own story of vulnerability to comfort him and feel empathy. It helps aloof person to open up and unburden his emotions and feelings. Whenever we interact, keep close check on what works and what makes them shy away.

JEALOUSY

Jealousy is an inevitable emotion that every one of us experiences. The problem with jealousy is that sometimes we do not get hold of it. It is alarming to experience what happens when jealousy overpowers thinking, and the way we feel about ourselves and people around us. Need is to understand where jealous feelings actually come from and learning how to deal with it.

One way is to look to jealousy originating from lower self-esteem. Many of us are often obsessed with self-critical thoughts about ourselves. It perpetuates negative thoughts and feelings, driving us to compare, evaluate and judge ourselves. This is one reason why learning how to deal with jealousy is so important. The situation may not be as damaging as we think and make out of it. In fact, our thoughts tell us about our situation is difficult to cope with. It is a basic reality that relationships go smoother when people do not get overly jealous. The more we can get a hold on our feelings of jealousy and make logic of them separate from other person, the better off we will be. A rejection or betrayal from other person is painful, but what often hurts us even more are the thoughts accumulated reminding about ourselves after the event. Our jealousy often comes from insecurity that broods a feeling like we are doomed to be deceived, hurt or rejected. Unless we deal with this feeling, we are likely to fall victim to feelings of jealousy, distrust or insecurity in any relationship, no matter what the circumstances.

These negative feelings originate from experiences in our lives. The most common manifestations of jealousy include fear, deep insecurity, constant worries, and envy. And very often people try to hide or mask it. That is why it is sometimes hard to tell if someone is being jealous of us or not. We feel jealous at times because of our sense that a cherished connection we have with another person is threatened by someone else. Think about type of thoughts do these jealous feelings spark and its deeper implications on mind.

Jealousy comes out of a lack of trust in your partner, friend, family member, close relative or in yourself. Lack of trust breeds insecurity, which creates jealousy. We supress these feelings because they are uncomfortable. When insecurity in our relationships is booming, jealousy rapidly grows and threaten to destroy the very relationship we are most afraid to lose. It is difficult to nurture any relationship while continuing with jealousy. How we use feelings is very important to our level of satisfaction and happiness.

If feelings assist our inner faults that finds self in low esteem compared to other person that is a destructive pattern with disturbing effects. It is healthy, to allow ourselves to have a competitive thought. However, if we deliberate or twist this thought into a criticism of ourselves or an attack on another person, we wind up getting hurt. These overreaction or feelings of envy creates jealousy.

The hallmark trait of being secure with yourself is loving who you are. If you are comfortable with yourself, you do not feel envious of another person's possessions and success. Whether your colleague or friends is successful ahead of you, it should not matter and feel you jealous as each person has his own ups and downs. One person's success does not mean you are failing. People who are secure with who they are, let go of any bitterness and focus on joy. They want everybody to be happy and successful.

CHAPTER SEVENTY-NINE

COMMUNICATION

We are required to communicate with others while in profession or in personal life. Depending on how we communicate with others, either it creates confusion and distrust or helps in building a cordial relationship. Communication can help to foster a good working relationship with our colleagues and customers, which can in turn improve efficiency. Effective interpersonal communication skills such as listening skills, making eye contact gives boost to our personality.

Communication is also about listening politely. It is the ability to offer empathy, open-mindedness, and helpful feedback based on what we hear. Also, a quality feedback will help in developing relationship with others. The ability to communicate effectively plays a large role in resolving conflicts and preventing potential ones from arising. Make sure all parties are heard and find a solution that is ideal for everyone involved. The most important aspect of effective communication is to treat others with respect, tolerate difference, control our emotions, ignore minor irritants while communication with others. One has to be very clear about the issues involved along with supporting data for the effective communication. It needs encouraging others to give feedback and not to discard their views outright. Involve other people in decision making. In this manner, communication is helpful to create an environment of mutual trust. Apart from the benefit it provides to other person with whom we are in communication, it helps us to remain in peace and out of conflict while dealing with others.

The communication at work place ought to provide clear expectations and objectives to your team members. They will understand their specific tasks and responsibilities, as well as those of their teammates, which will help eliminate conflicts and confusion. With effective communication, we can increase engagement, and thus boost satisfaction, among all the people dealing with us. With improved communication, team members will be better able to rely on each other. Communication skills can play an important role in nurturing positive work experiences for entire team. As people feel listened to and understood by you, it naturally improves work environment. Thus need is to have two way communication. Your juniors ought to be given adequate opportunity to express their views and feelings.

Good communication improves relationships with friends and family members. We have to be aware about facts and data before communicating with other person. Listening carefully and offering sincere feedback helps people to feel heard and understood. This, in turn, nurtures mutual respect. However, these days due to preoccupation with so many activities, we often lose patience to listen to others and fail to communicate properly. This usually happens in the family relation with our loved ones. We stretch our point of view too far and fail to reciprocate with love and compassion. Hence, personal life of so many of us is turning to be stressful and main reason behind is failure to communicate properly. Need is to introspect and find modification desired in our communication to be acceptable by others. Whether, it is proper poise to indicate respect for other person or patience to listen other person. If we pre-decide on the issue leaving no scope for any alternative, thereby not prepared to listen to other person. Is our superiority complex coming in our way to be polite to others who are perceived to be junior or lower in status? We notice certain mental blocks acting hindrance to effective communication. Getting rid of these will augur well for our peace and calmness.

CHAPTER EIGHTY

SUCCESS

While people crave for success, it is desirable to have understanding of all aspects that can limit potential for success. Defeat creates pain, inner turmoil and undermines self-esteem, and becomes source of unhappiness, worry and irritation. More than often, people believe that they can do something to succeed without being fully aware about it. They get into this belief by looking to other person. If someone else has achieved something, it makes them to believe that they are also capable to do it. This craze for success comes often without fully understanding the trouble to be taken to achieve it. How many people lead into a wrong profession, a bad marriage alliance or in a bad situation; thereafter finding it extremely difficult to come out only because they had false notion about their capabilities and understanding of others. Success have many dimension, a person may be successful in one aspect of life but may be found lacking in other aspect. A person should look to his competencies to realize success. Everyone ought to make good attempt to be successful, as defeat shatters self-esteem. Understanding own capabilities and improving on these is the most important aspect to move ahead in life with less of turmoil.

People who are successful have learnt to not blame others. Hope is a strong antidote to failure. A person who keeps hope is an eventual successful person. Lot of planning and hard work goes behind any success. If we do not have self-confidence then probably we will be too shy of presenting our ideas and may give up as soon as someone finds any fault. One needs to take some risk to realize goals. To increase chances of being a successful person, it requires self-confidence.

Efforts to being successful are worth taking. But the type of success we chose and the efforts that are made ought to be in tune with high personal and moral values. If the successes we desire are in conflict with strong values in life, even after being successful, we will be far off from real success. People often chose and focus on success in life based on momentarily comforts, false prestige and high ego. They devote lot of time in accomplishing the chosen success, but even then feel lot of inner turmoil and dissatisfaction. The real success is to prove useful to others and to society in addition to deriving personal and emotional comforts.

Success should not be accomplished using tactical and manipulative measures.

The most important aspect of success is how we live our life. If we have adopted good actions, tried to treat others with love, respect and devoted our time to constructive manner; it is living a useful life. Being either successful or unsuccessful ought not to haunt too much. It spoils inner condition.

Real success is one which is in tandem with reality. All other successes in life are secondary and temporary in nature. We ought to make full efforts to be successful in our profession, accumulating wealth and to maintain good relations, but not to bog down too much on the outcome of our efforts. We will taste success in one aspect while may face trouble some where else. It is therefore better to develop inner resolve to be successful in chosen areas which are in tandem with right and suitable course of life. Irrespective of whether eventually we succeed or not, but the satisfaction of having pursued the right path provides a feeling of success.

CHAPTER EIGHTY-ONE

HOBBY

Hobby is a regular activity for enjoyment, typically during leisure time, and not for gain of profession and remuneration. Hobbies include engaging in creative and artistic pursuits, playing sports, or pursuing other amusements. Hobbies can be physical or mental activities. When we are doing something we love and not for any other reason, it provides a feeling of excitement and joy. Hobbies break up routine and provides an outlet for taking up challenges without the stress that comes from a work-related issues. Adding another activity might seem to create more stress, but engaging in a new hobby provides outlet for releasing stress. Instead of worrying about the future or dwelling on the past, it is preferable to spend time on the particular hobby in the present.

Spending time on activities that we enjoy can help improve mental health and wellbeing. Research shows that people with hobbies are less likely to suffer from low moods, stress and depression. Activities like listening to music and spending time on a hobby is an effective way of managing stress. Engaging in creative activities such as writing, knitting, visual art and musical performance have all been shown to increase positive moods. Time spent towards creative activities produce positive emotions. Team sports offer important opportunities for social relationships, friendship, and support that can contribute greatly to mental health. Experience through sports or musical hobbies enhance enjoyment and help us feel less isolated. The key to finding a hobby and falling in love with it is to find favourite past-time.

Some hobbies have disadvantages, may lead to a waste of time and loss of the money. If someone loves to do something as a matter of hobby which eventually destroys him is not a good hobby. It is addiction and we lose control on self. Hence, playing video games, going to club may lead to addiction.

Meditation is a way to calm mind and connect with the Creator. We all need a healthy distraction that takes our thoughts off negative problems or challenges. Also, hobbies can improve mental alertness and concentration. Having such hobby is a great way to spend spare time and unwind from daily routine.

When we are passionate about our work, it is difficult to turn it off at the end of the day. Our mind remains engrossed with the work and it is difficult to avoid distraction from such thought. If we ever do step away from the actual work, ideas still float around in our mind. We may even find that thoughts of work distract mind also during sleep. While, in some ways, it is pleasing to be so consumed with work, it can also be exhausting. Engaging in some hobby will help in diverting mind from work related issues.

No matter how much we enjoy job, we need to have other things in life too. It is easy to ignore family, friends, hobbies, exercise, when we find joy at work. However, our job may not be able to provide long term enjoyment, we need to divert mind to various activities that appear enjoyable to us. Better to develop other outlets to energize self so as to find joy in all aspects of life. The choice of hobby need to be broad-based, it could be spending time with family, doing something together with family, going for a long walk, taking time off to visit some tourist place or simply relaxing. The purpose it to feel better and energized.

CHAPTER EIGHTY-TWO

EXERCISE

People who take regular exercise feel less anxious and it reduces the effects of stress. This is due to the chemicals we release into our brain when we exercise. These include dopamine and serotonin which have the effect of generating a feeling of well-being and of a positive mood. Exercise makes us feel better about ourselves, boosts our self-confidence and gives us a sense of control over our bodies and minds. Body image and the way we look at ourselves are obviously at the core of these feelings, but it is a fact that regular exercise does increase our happiness and confidence. Exercising can mean different activities and different levels of intensity to different people. It is not simply the domain of the young. In fact, people over 60 years of age who have taken some kind of regular exercise tend to be more positive in their outlook on life, have lower blood pressure and tend to suffer less from anxiety and mood fluctuations. Most people despite being aware about benefits of exercise, avoid to make it a part of daily routine, blaming on lack of time. We have made our self too busy with undesirable activities like gossiping, watching TV and feel tired and stressed. It thus becomes difficult to get up early for exercise.

Exercise is also good for getting rid of frustrations. If we find a sport we enjoy, many of us will still have a competitive urge and this desire to win often enables us to take our frustrations out on our opponent, all with good intentions and in good spirit. It also offers a distraction from feelings of anger, frustration or fear or some other kind of negative emotion which we might allow to take hold of us, if we did not have exercise to keep our minds occupied. Happiness and confidence are often linked to the way we look and feel about ourselves; exercise helps us get into shape and to wear the type of clothes which we feel suits us best. It makes us healthier; reduces or even eliminates the stress that often comes associated with feeling ill; and makes our immune systems less susceptible to things such as colds and flu. It makes us feel and look good and plays a significant role in feeling happier and more confident about ourselves.

Different Yoga help in physical well being and inner condition. Rajya Yoga is a sort of meditation that helps to think within, reaches for our true nature, and attempts to go beyond the material world into real self (that is soul). It balances and aligns inner Self so that we realize what our purpose is beyond physical existence. By control of body, mind and emotions, through breathing and movement, it helps to acquire the necessary clarity to make the right choices in our life. Yoga improves the concentration level, helps in focusing on real issues and reduces distractions of mind. It provides freshness in our thought process. Rajya Yoga enables us to adapt daily activities to feed inner self. People start enjoying everything they do, when able to concentrate due to impact of yoga exercise. It produces changes in the parts of the brain that regulate stress and anxiety.

Exercise has been shown to reduce anxiety, improves brain function and protect memory and thinking skills. To begin with, it increases heart rate, which promotes the flow of blood and oxygen to brain. It stimulates the production of hormones that can enhance brain cells and to prevent chronic disease. Regular physical activity is especially important in older adults since aging promotes changes in brain structure, the energy depletion that occurs during exercise stimulates recuperative processes during sleep.

CHAPTER EIGHTY-THREE

DAILY ROUTINE

Observing daily routine provide structure and discipline in our lives. Children are generally asked to follow a particular routine so as to inculcate discipline. But, as we grow old, we tend not to follow on particular routine. Most of us have no idea what to do when we wake up, because we have not thought about creating any particular schedule. As a result, many people feel stressed, anxious and falling short of their goals and true potential. The answer lies in carefully designing a routine that works best for each of us, one which helps us be productive, and in control.

Most people perceive daily routine being boring and rigid. They live their lives in an impulsive manner. On the contrary, designing and adhering to a personal daily routine is the way to productivity and fulfilling our true potential. We all have both good and bad habits. These habits form part of routine that play out every day for us, without us even having to think. Sometime it is tough to stick to a healthy daily routine. Let us not feel bad if we know that some unhealthy habits have crept into our day. The important thing is to recognize them so that we can make a change.

As we look at our daily routine, we can see how it can have the power to push us to become whatever we like to achieve. On the other hand, these daily routine can keep us stagnating without any growth. By ignoring or paying no attention to our daily routine will make our lives continue to be the same. The first step to changing routine and rebuild the ones that are not serving us, is awareness. This is because they have some sort of an underlying thought patterns that need to be attended to first. We find some positive daily routine can lead to a healthier and happier life.

Time is the most precious asset at our disposal, because once lost, it is non-retrievable. By following a routine, we free up time that would otherwise be spent on planning, decision-making and preparation. When we have a routine that we follow daily, it reduces the need to make decisions each day. It enables us to know exactly what tasks we need to do each day without having to contemplate, decide or think too much. When we are finished with one task, we know what comes next without much thought. Activities become standardized and we become more efficient as a result.

The beauty of designing a set routine is that it forces us to prioritize and decide what is important to us. It provides the framework within which we live our lives and conduct our daily activities. Daily routine may not work for all the time. Depending on the situation, we need to plan accordingly. Life is unpredicted and it is difficult to plan in advance. Hence, periodical review of the daily routine is required to adjust for changing environment.

High achievers tend to find routines that work for them, it is something they credit as a core to their success. Setting daily routine and following it helps to identify most important tasks in advance, before pressures of the day builds up. Ideally, the first few hours of each day should be spent conquering most challenging task. Similarly, a few moments at the end of the day to reflect on activities into proper perspective and sets agenda for the coming day. Setting daily routine is a step towards improving productivity, onset to deriving satisfaction in life.

CHAPTER EIGHTY-FOUR

MEMORY

Memory is the faculty of the brain where information is stored and retrieved when needed. It is the retention of information over time for the purpose of inducing future action. Human memory involves the ability to both preserve and recover information that have been learned or experienced. The ability to access and retrieve information from long-term memory allows to use these memories to make decisions, interact with others, and solve problems. Sometimes memories compete with one another, making it difficult to remember certain information. It is thus desirable to keep brain healthy by exercising regularly, maintaining social connections and managing stress that have been proven to help boost memory.

The moment we wake up in the morning, we should tell ourself to think on what is good for us; and on things that are beneficial to us. In this way, we will not clutter mind with things that will only make us confused and tired. Usually, these thoughts are about things that are pertaining to the future and some of these may not even happen to us at all. Worrying about the future by recalling bad moments of the past are the real enemies of peace of mind.

These days, we are overwhelmed by the overload of information. It keeps mind busy and tired. We are finding it difficult to relax. To reverse the trend, we have to first limit the level of information that is required and discard unwanted information. The unwanted information that remains in the form of memory has its impact on retaining calmness. We can start by scheduling a "quiet time" each day, before work or after work, to simply turn off all the external sounds and promptings and relax.

We have lots of memory stored in our brain that we can recount at any given moment. We can recall names, faces and places, but over time, these memories diminish as time passes and as we mature. Someone tries to forget memories that were painful. This is the way to move ahead with peace of mind. However, it may not be possible for all of us as bad memories lives with us in the form of behavioural patterns. We all move ahead with imprints of past experiences (good and bad) stored in our brain. Most of us do not know how to release them because we do not realize they exist. You may feel body tense up when you have to ask for help or borrow money, or your face may get hot when you are asked to speak in front of a crowd. It is remembering a past experience when you asked for help and it did not go well. The body does not have words to express itself, so it responds with physical sensation.

When we feel emotionally triggered to some addictive behaviour for comfort, it does not make us a bad person. It requires time to heal it. The healing process will bring up lots of different feelings and emotions; many will be uncomfortable. When these uncomfortable emotions and memories come up, allow them to come up without becoming attached to them. This will allow us to respond objectively. To get rid of our bad emotions and memory, exercise or write about these emotions. There will be times when exercise helps, and other times singing or writing will be more effective. The most important is to realize that bad memory is a baggage that is harmful for our well-being. The sooner we get rid of these, better it will be for our peace of mind. Need is to engage in positive activities that develops love, compassion, friendship so that we do not sit to brood over the past memory found harmful.

CHAPTER EIGHTY-FIVE

SENSITIVITY

A sensitive person is one who respects own and other person's feelings' and thinks deeply before speaking. It means taking the time to absorb and process, rather than rushing to a decision. For most of the people, being sensitive is not just a short -lived attitude, it is a key part of their personality. Sensitivity is often seen as a weakness, especially when such person is under stress. Easily stunned by plight of others, such person tend to get passionate and need to escape the stressful environment. Sensitivity is perhaps the most underrated quality. It is too often associated with fragility and weakness when it is also of tremendous strength. Sensitive people are astute and intelligent enough to recognize and comprehend their own emotions.

Everyone hates violence and cruelty on human and animals, but for sensitive people, seeing or hearing about it can be troubling. A sensitive person is able to immediately sense the moods of the people as they become aware of refinements like facial expressions, body language, and tone of voice that others may miss. These people have high level of empathy towards others. As a result, sensitive people tend to suffer from frequent emotional exhaustion. While being sensitive may be helpful for others, but getting obsessed to play events over and over in mind spirals into anxious thoughts. A sensitive person prefers to withdraw to a quiet environment in order to lower motivation level to soothe emotions and get recharge. They feel disgusted with the way things are and about their role in all of it. This being the reason that any change, both positive and negative impacts such person. They need more time than others to adjust to change.

Being sensitive is a good thing, as it alerts you to danger; it is also the basis for empathy. Sensitivity can lead either to empathy and/ or personal distress. Sensitivity can create anxiety, alarm or worry. Hence, one need not to be sensitive to the extent of creating personal distress. Let us remember that we can help others within our own limitation. One ought to be sensitive to take care of own feelings first and maintain required calmness. Those who feel empathy towards others rather than personal distress are more likely to be turned towards the needs of others. The possibility is that highly sensitive person may feel overwhelmed by what needs to be done in order to alleviate the sorrows of the other person.

The more we multitask, the more exhausted we become. The brain get exhausted when we are doing too much. The need is to set boundaries and place limits on our commitments to others. Saying no can be very difficult for sensitive person, because we feel guilty when we disappoint others. Since we feel everything so deeply, it is important for sensitive people to take time to reflect and sort emotions on a regular basis. Being over sensitive to other people's feelings, it creates guilt feeling for not able to help other person. Being critical with ourselves will only keep us trapped.

Let us understand that all the problems cannot be handled by us. We can be sensitive to the extent able to handle the issues. We are not responsible for all the problems, and will not be in position to sort. There is no point in getting over sensitive and brood continually on these issues. Better to pick up activities depending on own resources and capability. We have to create sensitive feelings in a positive manner. This way it brings overall calmness.

CHAPTER EIGHTY-SIX

DESIRES

Desire is a strong feeling that urges to the attainment or possession of something. While immersed in a pleasing fantasy, unconscious desires can be effortlessly realized. Some desire can actually be quite a good and necessary part of being human. The desire for knowledge, the desire to help others, the desire for a better life, the desire to become enlightened are all very powerful drivers to fulfil your ambition. Without desire, a person will not be motivated to work and achieve something in life. Without desire, life is meaningless, colourless, without purpose. From desire comes aspiration, achievement and accomplishment. Desire keeps us alive, and brings new life into being. We all want to be desired.

Desires for certain physical objects will temporary satisfy but lead to dissatisfaction in the long run. Keep them under control will not be harmful, as it energizes to perform better. As we meet one type of physical desire, our associated desires will increase and affect peace of mind and contentment. It has been observed that the desires of mind are greedy and they never get over because it is a vicious circle in which one desire end and other begins. So, it is extremely necessary to curb this unfavourable tendency of mind in the beginning to be really happy and peaceful in life.

However, not all the desires are bad especially the ones which are intellectual and aimed towards self-improvement and development, actually these are the desires that should be replaced by physical and emotional ones, as these are essential for us to prosper in life. Let us have desires to become better than others, more successful, wise, and knowledgeable than others. This is to cultivate higher intellectual desires instead of lower physical ones. If we can sow the seed of highest form of desire that is spiritual desire, in the presence of spiritual desire all other desires extinguish and only one burning desire remains which is to become self-sufficient in all means and attain supreme peace of mind. If we still cannot pacify the desires of the mind then we should satisfy desires in moderation and learn to bring contentment in life.

Desire is not the enemy to a happy and balanced life. When desire is driven by the self-esteem and sensory pleasures that is when it undermine our happiness and our well-being. The desire to win at any cost, the desire for better products, the desire for sexual fulfilment when it is destructive, these are examples of when desire is allowed to override logic or love or respect. It is at this moment that desire becomes harmful to others and to yourself. The time we are struck with the notion of desire for something, ask where it is coming from. If you are the only one who will be helped, then control ego before it starts driving your desire. If there are no limits to our desires, which is a sure sign it is our ego again. Our ego is ending in its drive, and it will drive us to misery in order to be satisfied.

It is to ponder whether our desires are more to satisfy our self ego and sensory pleasures. It may be difficult to curb these desires bringing pleasures initially. It is difficult to keep these desires under control and person becomes addicted to such desires. The need is to think to curb such desires at the beginning, and concentrate and devote time to other activities that enrich yourself as a person. Let us ask self where the limits to our desires lay. Make sure the "more" that we want is in line with the person we want to become. Only then we find peace in life.

CHAPTER EIGHTY-SEVEN

SACRIFICE

People are generally selfish in nature. They wish to take care of own self-interest even at times at the cost of others. However, as people develop inner capabilities to love, respect and feel compassionate towards others, it makes them to take care of others as much as they look after self-interest. This single act makes people to be straight forward, truthful, and considerate towards others. A step further towards taking care of other, demands sacrificing own needs for the benefit of other people. It is noble act and in tune with inner urge.

Sacrifice means suffering some loss for the benefit of another person. It is a pious act to give more to someone at the cost of own inconvenience. Sacrifice is being willing to give up something good for something better. Life is full of boundless possibilities, but in order to transform a possibility into a reality we have to choose -- sacrificing something in order to attain the one. Nothing is gained without something relinquished. Sacrifice has meaning only in the context of a goal, dream or mission. In pursuing these, we often face obstacles which require us to forfeit physical or emotional comfort in the service of something that matters more. Often, the greater the dream or vision, the greater the shared sacrifice required to attain it. Sacrifice is easier when we stay focused on what we are choosing rather than what we are giving up.

Sacrifice is not suffering in real sense. People treat sacrifice and suffering in similar context; it is the reason people desist act of sacrifice. Everyone has lot of things that they can sacrifice for the benefit of other person without self suffering for these possessions. Wealthy person can part with some wealth, a knowledgeable person his knowledge, and a courageous person his physical support. In sacrificing something, we are actually gaining something else. A wealthy person receives respect from other person, knowledgeable person gains further in knowledge and a courageous person gains further in his courage. Nothing can create profound impact than acts of sacrifice. Through the acts of sacrifice, it is to bring the inner connection with other people and God as no other way will be equally effective. This is the reason that people who wish to move ahead in their spiritual pursuit look for the acts of sacrifice. Look to your inner self; it shows extreme level of happiness and peace with each act of sacrifice.

Despite material sacrifice and inconveniences in attending to someone, you still feel happy and satisfied. Making a promise to someone is one of the most influential forms of communication. Still, many times we make vows that we do not possibly keep. We put faith in promises to help us negotiate conflicts, solve problems and commit to love and enter into relationship. However, for most of us, when it comes to the promises that we make each day, we usually break more than we keep. Breaking promises not only disappoints the person we have promised, but it also erodes our self-esteem. It may be difficult to keep our word exactly as promised as sometimes business and circumstances undergo change beyond our control. As God has been kind to us to provide us wealth, knowledge and other comforts, it ought to make us to sacrifice part of it to the benefit of other person. This is why so many organizations are engaged to donate and serve the society. Taking a broader picture in view, act of sacrifice brings you close to reality and oneness with others. Other people feel gratitude towards you. In serving other people, you serve HIM. Small acts of sacrifice are good to keep you close to real goal in life.

JUDGEMENTAL

Human nature is to sit on judgement about other people. We have developed the habit to analyse other person and to find some fault and judge him based on his weakness. If opportunity comes, we make a fun of the person. At the back of our mind is to prove that we are better placed. We see someone, and based on their looks or actions, pass judgment on them. We do not make an effort to get to know the person, or understand them, or see whether our judgment was right or not. We see something they do, and get angry, or disappointed or think worse of them. We judge, without understanding, and do not try to find out more about the person through communication. That takes time and effort, but taking that extra effort does make difference in judging others. Better avoid passing judgment and instead build a connection between two human beings. This will reduce pain as no need is to justify your judgement.

The first step towards avoiding judging others and passing adverse comments is to observe our thoughts for a few days, trying to notice when we are being judgmental. Once we are aware, try to stop when we feel being judgmental. Instead of judging someone for what he has done or how he looks, try instead to understand the person. Try to imagine the circumstances that might have led to the person acting or looking like they do. Accept that person for who he is, without trying to change him. Each individual is different and we can only change a little bit of the person. Hence, it is better to accept and love the person for who he is, and by this way it will serve to make us happier. It can be life-changing.

Too much judgement has a negative effect on our thoughts, emotions and even physical health. It leads to anxiety, anger and anguish resulting in health problems. In this way, judgement prevents you from living a healthy lifestyle that is full of well-being, joy and peace. Take note of your thoughts and the things you say. Be aware of the times when you are being overly critical, and ask yourself why you feel this way. Are your thoughts rooted in reality, or are they coming from a place of fear and insecurity. Once you notice yourself being judgemental, you can take actions to reverse this self-destructive behaviour. When you make an effort to find the good in people, you train your mind to be compassionate and caring. In this way, you nurture your heart and create a positive energy that will benefit not only yourself, but everyone around you.

Sometimes all it takes is a slight shift in thinking to turn judgement into positive thinking. The way we speak to self internally has everything to do with how our life moves ahead. Our thoughts decide course of action. The people who spend a significant time together tend to pick up each other's characteristics and behaviour. Hence, we should avoid friends or acquaintances who are critical and judgemental of themselves and other people. It can impact our thought process. Try to surround yourself with positive people with good energy. Try to be kind to yourself and the people around you.

Take note of instances when you have been critical of others. Realize that it is futile to find fault of others as we are not fully aware about other person. A decent way to do this is to love and make note of this warm, loving emotion and feel it overtakes you. If you project this feeling out to others, you will notice others are kinder to you in return, and you will be more peaceful.

CHAPTER EIGHTY-NINE

RELATIONSHIP

An ideal relationship is one that remain strong even after having ups and downs. Relationship is often referred in the context of family, friendships and other acquaintances. People in ideal relationships work hard to communicate and avoid misunderstandings. All of us hanker for ideal relationship so as to remain in joy and happiness. Our expectation from other person remains high. We like to receive love, respect and attention from other person in relationship. More often, people face difficulty in maintaining cordial relationship which becomes cause for stress, anxiety and pain. It is often difficult to live in love with our spouse and other family members despite material comforts.

The relationship is all about mind management. If we are not able to control negative emotions, it will be difficult to maintain ideal relationship. Ideal relationship is based on compassion. People who are not able to treat others with compassion jeopardize the relationship.

Relation can be nurtured based on certain principles. It is to share with others what we possess. If we do not have anything of substance, then we will not be able to share with others. It does not mean mere material possessions, but love, compassion, empathy and sincerity. If we do not develop love and compassion in our heart, then it will not be possible to share these with others. First, we should possess all these attributes in abundance within us to be able to share with others. The basic premise is 'giving' in the relationship. We should have the capability and intention to give something in the relationship. It means that we have to develop our awareness to reach to other person so as to appreciate the true meaning of 'giving'.

Being able to share our emotions without feeling judged or devalued is what is required in the family relationship. You need to let each other know what you are thinking and feeling. We all need to learn how to accept each other and our circumstances, so we can move ahead in life together in a way that enhances our lives and relationships. Let us accept the realities of the present situation in life. It is only way we can move to the next level. Having a partner, creates a buffer between you and the difficulties in life. Let us be honest with each other about feelings and needs, and remember that you can tell the truth without being harsh. We have limited scope to change other person in the relationship.

In the process, we should learn to accept the weakness of the other person and not to make a big issue out of it.

Every successful relationship needs care and nurturing to each other in a way that creates a mutually beneficial connection. It requires to maintain a positive attitude. Being positive may be the key to remain in harmony. You can control your behaviour and even your moods when necessary, and having a loving partner who is willing to be there for you, even when you are struggling, make your relationship positive.

We ought to understand the true essence of 'giving' in a relationship. Only when we have the capability to give something to other person without expecting anything of substance in return, it builds relationship. Otherwise, relationship is mere play and will fall apart after we have become tired and bored of that play. All other means to attain ideal relationship will fall short of true purpose of relationship. Hence, we have to develop aptitude to engage in giving to others without expecting anything in return. It is a way to evolve to realize true purpose in life.

CHAPTER NINETY

OVER-ANALYSE

When we over-analyse a particular issue, we try to go into more detail and break the analysis into various components. We spend lot of time to look to pros and cons. It becomes difficult to come to a particular decision as mind remains bogged down with various data and its interpretation. In the process, small issue tend to become complicated and affects productivity. We lose confidence and fear and anxiety develops and makes us to further analyse. It goes like a vicious circle. Sometimes, a small issue becomes too much complicated and we spend lot of time on analysing it. It brings worry and stress at that moment. When we put things into a wider perspective, we realize that we are worrying too much and perhaps escalating the situation. The net impact is mind remain disturbed and we are not able to attend properly to various issues.

As we over-analyse things, it is because of lack of confidence. When we do not believe in self, we go on thinking negatively on the issue rather than looking to positive aspect. It can take a serious toll on our well-being. We brood on our shortcomings and mistakes, it increases health problems. As we overanalyse a situation, we are troubled by it and mind fails to think rationally. The solution to this problem is to pay more attention as how to control thoughts and feelings. We shall come to know when we over-analyse and why. Once we start to see it happening, we have to practise and divert mind out of it. Over-analysing everything interferes with problem-solving. It will cause us to stay on the problem rather than look for solutions. The main reason for over-analyse is lack of confidence. This way we feel stuck and often caught in a trap, and keep this cycle going.

When people over -think, it is usually their habit to go to the minutest details and analyse. A way that they can control things. There is nothing wrong up to a limit. It provides more clarity about the issue. However, depending on the importance of the issue, one need to spend time accordingly. If we spend lot of time and still find it difficult to come to a decision, it is counter productive and a matter of concern. Analysis is only a part of the whole problem, much depend on the implementation. We have to understand that situations change and have to quickly respond to these changes. We cannot control everything that happens to us, but need is to know how we react to it. When people over analyse, they usually will analyse every possible outcome in future, but as we realize that we cannot control the future, it may help to curtail our thoughts.

Stopping overanalyse helps in proper allocation of time to various activities, improves productivity and balance our different roles. We ought to allocate time for each activity depending on importance to be effective. You will not be engrossed in the analysis and find time to attend to your family and friends. You will not face dearth of time.

If we tend to be critical of self, it is likely to create negative thoughts finding it difficult to deal with certain situations. This will bring realization that we are not capable to do a job properly. The moment we do away the over- analyse, this inner chattering will stop and we can manage situation with confidence. All we need is a good distraction that can help stop over analysing. If there is a certain situation that seems to engage our mind a lot, try to distract mind by doing something else. Using these as a distraction can be helpful because this way we can feel a lot calmer, and may find it easier to quiet our thoughts.

CHAPTER NINETY-ONE

PREJUDICE

Prejudice stems from a deeper mental need to associate with a particular way of thinking. People who want to make quick decisions about a person are prone to not go into details and make generalization. When we meet someone, we immediately see that person based on his nationality, caste, colour, creed, religion and race. We thus label the person with the characteristics belonging to that group which can be misleading and not based on any rational thinking. Social categories are useful to reduce complexity, but the problem is that we also assign some properties to these categories. Everyone has to make decisions, but some people quickly rely on the most obvious information. People who need to make quick judgments will judge a new person based on what they already believe about their category. This can lead to prejudice and stereotyping.

Prejudice is an unjustified attitude or opinion, usually a negative one, directed toward an individual. Prejudices are mostly irrational because they are not sufficiently based on experience, and lead to misjudgements and discrimination. When people are undervalued by others, their self-esteem suffers and they stop trying to improve themselves. Prejudice has a harmful effect on mental, social and physical well-being. Like the wide variety of prejudices that exist in societies, the consequences and the influence these have are also varied. Prejudice held by individuals is outcome of a false social status that strongly influences who they are, what they think, and even the actions they take. People who are perceived to be lower in social and economic status in the society are generally impacted adversely by these prejudices. People generally form a poor opinion of a particular person because of social set up and it takes lot of efforts by the aggrieved person to achieve his rightful position.

People acting out their prejudices cause violence and loss. Opportunities in life are lost and personal relationships damaged when people act upon their prejudice. When not acknowledged and confronted, prejudice negatively impacts the lives not only of the victims, but of those holding the prejudice. Our brain finds someone to blame, to find fault with, and to condemn. This kind of blame game can begin as a tiny feeling and soon grows big. It begins with a single, simple thought in the mind of one person that can escalate. The effect of prejudice is irrational fear and hate, the effect could be of violence and disharmony in the society.

To create internal resilience against prejudice is to look for facts based on your experience. Think whether your prejudice against other person is outstretched based on generalization. Acknowledge your experiences with others and derive meaning. A lot of people find meaning after understanding others. You may not be able to change other people, but have control to get rid of prejudice. Brooding prejudice against other person just because of different background and exterior appearance creates negativity. Hence, we will not be able to appreciate the goodness in that person and will not be able to develop close bonding. It will impact our broader perspective that is based on all beings have come from one source and need to be respected and have compassion towards all. Hence, external differences on account of different culture, custom and living habits ought not to make us ignore the generosity and goodness in other person. To live a life of peace and calmness is to ponder on all these issues and clear our mind from this dirt of prejudice.

CHAPTER NINETY-TWO

BLESSINGS

Blessing is something that is lucky and makes us feel happy. These are perceived to be gifts from God. We look for these blessings from God and pray for these to be showered on us and to others. We ought to be grateful to the blessings already with us. This may be wealth, status, loving family and good health. We feel these are the blessings from God and remain grateful. As we count on these blessings, it makes us to feel better and satisfied. Blessings is thinking about good things already with us and also praying for these to come to us in future. To remain peaceful, count on these blessings and be grateful all the time to God, even during adverse circumstances. However, rather than counting on these blessings, which are plenty; our tendency is to look for the blessings of others and feel jealous of them.

Blessings are nothing but positive vibes which is passed from elders to us. If you are going to respect and take care of elders, they bless you with good things to come in your life. Mother is a blessing of God in a human form. Having a mother is probably God's greatest boon in our lives. It is her love that make us strong, her care that prepare us to face the world, her hands that help us overcome all the trying times of life. We have to cherish these blessings.

The gifts we receive in the form of comforts, success, love and friendships are outcome of the blessings from God. We need to develop inner connection with God while recalling all these comforts as blessings. However, we are often hankering for pride, and do not value our blessings. Hence, we do not seek blessing of the higher order that is to create saintliness and love of the ultimate. Our life goes in seeking blessings of the worldly comforts.

We are blessed to bless others. So from our words and actions should flow blessings that encourage and value others. Loving others is the greatest of all blessings that we can ever give them. The love that flows from our heart to others is that which is poured into our hearts by the divine. We need not to hold on to this love but share with others by way of blessings. We do not have to wait to have abundance before we can share with others. Some of us grew up being encouraged to do others as we would like them to do to us. Not only would our lives be changed, but the lives of those to whom we interact would be positively impacted.

We bless others with good wishes to come from higher source i.e. God. 'To be blessed' means to be favoured by God, the source of all blessing. Blessings, therefore, are directly associated with, and are believed to come from, God. Thus, to express a blessing is like bestowing a wish on someone that they experience the favour of God. When we bless someone in family and friend, it is to think well and to wish that God will take care of them. As you engage in blessing others, it is to think good about the person. It brings positivity in our behaviour. Blessings to others should come genuinely from our heart and need not be merely symbolic. Our heart ought to feel to bless others.

The cardinal principle is to seek blessings from others and in return bless others. Do all that is required to seek blessings from elders, parents and others. It requires building up connection and to take care of them. However, blessings from others are not to be demanded. It should flow from others naturally out of love and compassion. Bless others with good wishes, love and compassion. Counting on these blessings is to remain positive, satisfied and peaceful.

CHAPTER NINETY-THREE

SOLITUDE

Solitude is a state of seclusion or isolation with people. It may stem from bad relationships, loss of loved ones, deliberate choice, mental disorders, employment or other situation. But solitary skills could be helpful to remain mentally stronger. People who set aside some time to be alone tend to be happier. They are not faced with problems when situation demands remaining alone. They know how to spend time gainfully while being alone. A person who practises solitude will get calmness. They report better life satisfaction and lower levels of stress. They are also less likely to have depression. Everybody in the busy schedule ought to get used to remain in solitude.

Solitude is generally looked as inconvenient, to be avoided, a sort of punishment, and often aligned with negative outcomes. This is especially true in times of personal turbulence, when the instinct is to reach outside for support. When people are experiencing crisis, at that stage moments of solitude, will help in learning about how to deal with some of the harmfulness that surrounds them in the society.

While spending time with people is good, but too much time in socializing might also be a bad thing. Solitude is an essential component to health and well-being. Building more solitude into daily life might actually reduce your feelings of loneliness. Solitary skills grow over time to be comfortable with being by yourself. There are many reasons to spend time alone as it can help build the mental strength to reach greatest potential. When you are by yourself, you can choose how to spend time without worrying about anyone else. Making choices on your own help to develop better insight.

Spending too much time with friends, family and colleagues often exhausts and amounts to wastage of time in gossip. Spending time alone breaks down those barriers. Studies show you will develop more compassion for other people when you set aside time for solitude. There is a reason artists, musicians, and authors seek solitude when they want to create something. Being alone often fosters creativity. In addition to boosting creativity, solitude also improves productivity. Solitary skills help become mentally stronger. You do not need to keep aside huge time in order to benefit from solitude, but few minutes of alone time each day could be enough to help rejuvenate from the daily routine.

It is important to have time for family and profession, it is equally useful to find time to living as an individual. Setting aside time to be alone can help reflect on your goals, dreams, and aspirations. If you think you do not have time to sit quietly and think, you probably need alone time more than ever. The busier you are, the more likely you are to benefit from some quiet time. Your dependence on others will come down.

The greatest advantage to practice solitude is to realize your inner self (soul). Hence, the time spent in solitude can be better utilized in remembrance of God. Whether you decide to meditate, or think about any issue, allow yourself to be alone with your thoughts. If you are not used to solitude, the silence and lack of activity can feel uncomfortable at first. But, setting aside time to be alone is an essential component of building mental strength and living a calm and peaceful life.

CONNECTION

Connection with family, relations, friends, colleagues and neighbours is important for our mental and physical well-being. It opens opportunity to know other person, help and care about him. By connecting with other person, it helps in knowing other person and in turn seek his cooperation. It works a protective factor against anxiety and depression. Strong ties with family, friends and the community provide us with happiness, security, support and a sense of purpose. People who feel more connected to others have higher self-esteem, greater empathy for others, are more trusting and cooperative; as a consequence, others are more open to trusting and cooperating with them.

The only connection that work well will be with ones that we truly care about. If we do not have a genuine interest in the person with whom are trying to connect, then it is better stop trying. Let us be kind but honest and share what we really feel. Instead of brooding on what someone else did wrong, it is to ask self what can be done to create the change we are seeking. Have fun with someone you love. Forget about everything that feels like a problem.

Too many people try not to connect with those perceived to be above them in status and prosperity, due to the fear that they would not be able to offer anything in return. Give real thought to who you could connect to benefit them to realize their goals. If it turns out that you cannot be that helpful, the gesture alone will stand out.

It is impossible to genuinely offer help if we do not pay attention. It requires going one step further to understand their business, background and passions. It requires investing time in learning what really matters to them and how you can help. Connecting with others requires going beyond casual interaction to understand them, as all of us have got different set of capabilities. These capabilities remain hidden and unexploited unless we connect with others. As people, be our relations, friends and neighbours become aware of self, it opens scope to connect and be useful to them. We visualize ourselves as useful.

Being connected has some benefits. It develops rapport with others and opens opportunity for personal growth.

People tend to know you and your capabilities and passion. As you know and help others, they may also reciprocate. When people refer you for a particular task or opportunity, it acts as a catalyst to move ahead. Spend more time connecting with your network of friends and colleagues and see where it leads.

Think how you have connected with others. Is the sole purpose of you getting connected with others is for some benefit. What is choice of people with whom you get connected? As you search answers, you may find that the primary aim is to derive some benefit from these connections. You may realize that this will not lead to far. Are they feeling comfortable in your company? Are you showing compassionate and empathy towards others? We have to ponder these issues and bring broader purpose of life to forefront through connection with others. Connecting with others serves a bigger purpose, to be helpful to others and in return provides satisfaction and peace. It all comes back to helping others. If we spent time thinking about how we can help everyone we come in contact with. We will find everything else takes care of itself. It makes us enjoy the companion of others and step towards attaining peace of mind.

CONTRIBUTION

Our Life is contribution to self and others. It is something you do together to help produce or achieve something with other people or to help make something successful. When you make a contribution, it means you are giving something away; whether it is your money, your possessions, or your time. A contribution can take many forms. As humans, we are driven to make our personal unique contribution in the world, and we can really accomplish something in this short lifetime. This will bring purpose and meaning to life. We will get satisfaction and it will keep us busy and away from boredom and negative emotions. As we contribute something for others, it enhances self-esteem, joy and peace in life.

We get caught up in comparison, thus evaluating our achievements against those of our family, friends and public figures. Most people are carried away by the trivial issues of life and thereby miss out on most important activities. What contribution we make out of our existence. Is it all about making money and enjoying the little time we spend here? Each individual is different. Our paths are different so we may not follow the same way to make the place we live better. It could be our knowledge, wealth, physical help, music, and some other trait that may offer as contribution to the society. All that matters is that we perform the task at hand with a good intention and purpose. In whatever we are doing, let us ensure to give best to it. In whatever field of life we are engaged, choose excellence. That is one way to contribute.

Let high standard and sincerity be allowed to guide us in all activities so as to enhance our contribution towards others. Leverage purpose to serve someone else, not for money. That means helping others pursue their passion, or motivating them to reach their goals. Whatever gives life meaning, give it to someone freely.

Contribution can be in different manner. Maybe you have a special talent, such as art or music or teaching young children. Perhaps you have a scientific mind or have leadership skills. Noticing and valuing your contribution on a daily basis can help you cope with the difficulties you experience.

The main purpose of contribution is to search for

broader purpose of life. Someone may seek this purpose in religion and getting attached to the activities that promote its faith. Faith and connection to spirituality gives a strong foundation for coping with whatever comes our way. You will suffer less from the judgments of others, if you know that your actions are not about you, but about what you are called to do. Life spent without any contribution to others is a waste.

One of the most effective ways of coping with daily ups and down is to know your purpose and contribution to the society. Every contribution for the betterment of society counts. Every person can make a difference. There are so many ways to contribute to others. We are all connected and the actions of each of us affect others. If you are not sure what your contribution is, then consider activities that you are passionate about. If we live a life full of compassion and empathy towards others, it itself will be contribution towards others. We may not be aware about it, but our words and actions will be of help to others. It will bring a peaceful environment.

TRUTH

Telling the truth is never easy, but truth as incredible power is a necessary constituent for a fulfilling life. It is not only beneficial for the person who is telling the truth, but also for the person who is told the truth. Most of the time, we slightly distort the truth in order to manipulate people around us. Because when we tell the truth we give up power to control people around us. We fear that telling truth could reduce our tactic and expose us. This may be due to lack of courage to face the consequences on account of telling the truth. Several reasons may be attributed to escape telling the truth but the most prolific one among them is the materialistic ambitions leading to mania of acquiring name, fame, wealth and power by hook or by crook. Truth is perceived to be coming as hindrance to these ambitions.

Truth is something like perpetual source of power and energy, provider of self-confidence, remover of fear and suspicion, a generator of courage, infinite, eternal, unshakable that never gets eroded. To hide one lie, one has to tell a series of lies and even then it is not certain that the lie shall remain under cover forever. In view of the above why not we start practising truth in all walks of our life. It sounds hypothetical but not absurd or impossible.

No change is impossible without knowing the truth. How can people around us change if they are not told the truth? However, instead of telling the truth, we often hide it because we do not like to upset others. Deep down we do not want to be rejected. We refuse to give people the freedom to reject us or to get angry at us and want to control them. By being true to others, you become a better friend, partner, parent or colleague. Real love comes on practising truth. Lack of truth will lead to the decay of any relationship. When others perceive you as someone who is telling the truth, they will seek your advice and listen to you. They will respect you for that. Accepting to tell the truth to people means that you are willing to fully express your feelings no matter how scary it is. It clearly shows a high level of trust and encourages your family, your friends, your partner or other people you are interacting with to open their heart too.

Truth is power. Let us learn to use it to bring more

integrity in our life. Remember that truth might often be painful to hear, and learn to deliver it in a way so that other people do not get defensive. Truth that comes from a place of love and consideration will be appreciated. The inner consciousness (soul) is a form of divine energy that flows in all living bodies. This divine energy is nothing but Love. This love cannot be created unless people abide by certain virtues of highest order like sincerity, humility, truth, contentment, gratitude and compassion. The Truth is wordless and cannot be explained.

Practising Truth may be difficult initially, but as we go ahead it bestows inner calmness. In this case, we have not to struggle to hold on to the lie. This ultimate Truth is the realization of divinity within us. We have to practice truth in ordinary life and make it as true identity of yourself to eventually know the Ultimate Truth. Being true allows you to maintain a high level of integrity and brings peace of mind. You know that you are living a life that is in line with higher values. This is moving one step towards divinity.

CHAPTER NINETY-SEVEN

FAITH

Faith is trust in someone and his ability; in the existence of God; in the doctrines of teachings of religion or any other thing as a code of ethics or morality. Faith is thus a belief that is not based on proof but on trust. Faith develops obligation, reliability and devotion to a person, promise or engagement.

Faith, at its core, is deep-rooted in the expectation of good things to come. When we believe in God, it develops faith that God will take us out of the difficult situation. It energizes us and negative thoughts are subdued. It goes beyond hope. While much of hope lives in the mind, faith is deep in the heart and the spirit. Faith brings positivity and connection with the ultimate. It is a pray and dialogue with inner self (soul) for bringing good things in life. When mind loses hope and feels dejected, it is faith that drives us to move ahead in life despite difficulties. It does not hold any logic. It cannot be explained or be understood through a single dimension. While life can be hard at the best of times, faith is the knowledge, deep down inside, that believes that things will get better. It is beyond our comprehension.

Even when situation seemed dire and bleak, it is faith that carries us through. It is based on our deepest wishes and desires. Unfortunately, some people do not believe in things that they cannot see. The mind is an incredibly powerful tool. In times of trouble, mind tend to move away from positivity. But, faith is the tool that helps replenish abundance in the heart and the spirit, not just in the mind. If we focus on problems, we live solely in those problems and have difficulty moving past the negativity. When we have abundant faith; it trains our minds to think of good things, and we gravitate towards that. We attract good things because we believe and expect good things to come. Similarly, when we believe and expect bad things to come, we also attract that into our lives.

Going through life and all of its ups and downs, it is enough to question our very existence. But through all of the trials and tribulations, it is faith that gives us that helping hand. It works to guide us in the right direction, moving us towards and allowing us to discover our purpose in life. Usually, when we are faced with a difficult situation, it gets harder before it gets better.

Little by little, a part of us is broken, until one day, we dig deep down inside and somehow find the strength we needed to make it through. That strength comes from our faith. It is the guiding light that helps push us towards our purpose.

No matter what the situation is, no matter how bad or dire you think it might seem, your faith can and will get you through it. You must accept that as fact, and hold on to the expectation of greater things to come. If you really want something in life, and I mean you really want it deep down inside and you have a strong-enough reason you absolutely must achieve it, faith is the thing that helps you to see that through.

It's easy to allow stress, anxiety, and fear to ruin our lives. Sometimes, these worries manifest into highly-stressful situations, causing both mental and physical problems. But faith helps to keep those things at bay. Even when we have no reason to believe that things will get better, it's through faith that situations do improve. When we hold the expectation of good things to come, no challenge is too difficult. Faith helps to eliminate stress, anxiety and fear.

CHAPTER NINETY-EIGHT

TOLERANCE

Tolerance is willingness and ability to accept feelings, habits, or beliefs that are different from our own. Tolerance is an important trait that helps people to live together peacefully. It means that you do not put your opinions above those of others, even when you are sure that you are right. Tolerant people show strength in that they can deal with different opinions and perspectives. Tolerant people tend to ignore small irritants so as to remain in positive frame of mind and enjoy joy and happiness in life. These people realize that being tolerant is helpful to achieve broader purpose of life and not to get stuck in brooding about bad things happening in life. Tolerance does not come easily. Mind needs to be disciplined as not to react immediately but pause and listen carefully and respect other person even during disagreement. We have to control emotions and believe that there is no perfect solution to any problem. Hence, the views and suggestions of others need not be discarded and rejected outright.

Being able to accept different view from other person can have positive effect on our well-being. It removes self-imposed barriers and allows one to think more broadly and enjoy greater inner peace. Tolerance leads to less stress and greater happiness within your society.

The way to develop tolerance is to listen carefully without jumping to conclusions and try to understand the other person's point of view and agree to disagree. Let us not have a pre-conceived notion that we are always right and our point of view to be accepted. In this situation, we do not have capacity to tolerate others. How often we lose our temper and develop negative emotion of anger and hate on very trivial issues, simply because we did not practised tolerance. Being tolerant does not mean to necessarily have to compromise principles or embrace or accept others' ideas. It is to remain tolerant even when we decide to disagree. In this manner, other person is expected to show tolerance towards us. A person might fully disagree with others on any issue, from religion to politics, while at the same time honouring and respecting those with different ideas and opinions and treating them with full dignity and honour.

Tolerance is needed in all spheres of life, and on every level and on every stage, because it plays a vital role to establish peace and love, from the smallest unit up to the highest unit of society. Learning to be tolerant and respectful of others is key to being successful in life. If tolerance leads to acceptance and understanding, then intolerance breeds innumerable negative issues. Intolerance breeds due to religious or cultural differences. We have to learn to live with others despite diversities. It would be possible if we understand and appreciate other person's culture and beliefs.

It is a moral obligation or duty which involves respect for the individual as well as mutual respect and consideration between people. Tolerance between people makes it possible for conflicting claims of beliefs, values and ideas to coexist as long as they fit within acceptable moral values. When tolerance is placed within the moral domain relating to fairness, justice and respect and avoiding causing harm to others, it can only be viewed as a positive virtue retaining calmness and peace while dealing with other person.

CHAPTER NINETY-NINE

RIGHT OR WRONG

What is right or wrong depend on specific situation and personal judgment. Telling lie is an action generally considered to be wrong by moral standard. A killer asks about whereabouts of your neighbour with intention to harm and murder him. What a person will do in this situation. Hold on to truth and allow your neighbour to be robed of his valuables and life. I do not think anybody will face dilemma in telling lie in this situation. Despite the fact that people advocate telling truth is a virtue, telling a lie in this particular case is the right thing to do. It achieves the higher moral value of protecting the life of your neighbour.

Hence, a right or wrong action cannot be viewed in isolation. It depends on circumstances and underlying purpose. Every individual based on his teachings and understanding has the capability to know what is right or wrong. It depends on what a person aspires in life. Our actions can go wrong due to lack of awareness and understanding. We may not like to be seen as wrong; it impacts self ego. Instead of changing and improving on doing things differently and rightly, the tendency is to justify our action as right. This impulse to be right at all the times is root cause of wrong doing. The problem gets further murkier when we think that other person dealing with the situation differently is wrong.

A person wishes to be seen as right in front of others. Despite certain weakness, it has become habit of so many people to deem themselves right in all situations. The attempt is to misrepresent the fact, adopt tactical representation and put blame on others to divert the attention from the wrong action. These days corruption, kickbacks and other favours are common in various business deals. Those who indulge in it try to justify it as special privileges for being in that position of power. Professionals charge exorbitant fees for the services offered by them and try to justify it as price for their expertise. If we look to the moral values, charging something exorbitant is not a right thing. A person who is sympathetic and have empathy towards others will not take undue advantage of other person.

What is right or wrong depends on so many factors and need not to be looked merely from the legal perspective but search the higher purpose that underlies any action. So many actions may be within the laid down laws of the country, but still these may be selfish and not doing well to others. Any action will be deemed to be right if it does well to other person. One has to be very discreet in his judgment to deem someone as wrong. We will be doing lot of harm to someone by labelling that person as wrong without understanding fully the circumstances.

Any decision has two aspects; one that fulfils immediate need of body and other that looks to fulfilling inner consciousness. A person who is fully conscious of his physical self, will be giving priority on self-interest that looks for gain, reward, comforts, and material possessions, Another person who is conscious of meeting his inner need will also look for love, compassion, sincerity, honesty and peace. Now, most of us are not fully conscious of inner self (soul), hence this dilemma will continue as whether to give priority to meet physical need or also take care of inner self. There is no absolute right and wrong, rather it varies in degree. In such situations, the best way to decide about right thing to do is to pick one which fulfils higher purpose of life. It is the way to bring peace and fulfil higher purpose of life.

RELEVANCE OF DEATH

Life is a form of consciousness. Once body loses this consciousness, it is deemed dead. This consciousness is beyond body and mind. We are not able to comprehend about this consciousness during our life time because we treat body and inner consciousness as the same. This consciousness is controlled by someone who has the power to give and take it from human body. As our normal sensory organs and science have not been able to reveal full mystery of this force, it is imperative to think of role of God in our birth and death. We may assign various reasons for death from medical perspective, but these are only periphery causes while the real role is spiritual.

Why God will like a person to come in this world and then die. Believing on reincarnation indicates that death is not end of our existence. It is to move from one life to another. Hence our real-self is in present life and many lives earlier and more lives in future. The cruelty of death gets diluted when people think of it as a transitory stage of total existence. Who knows the death would have been conceived as an opportunity to understand the life itself. If a person remains in same condition, he gets little opportunity to learn and rectify his wrong doing. From divine perspective death, is an opportunity to come out from a particular situation and be in new environment.

The real self is the same, but only body consciousness (Ego) has been replaced with the new set of body consciousness. It is therefore logical to think that everything of the past cannot be washed away as we are to bear the rewards and punishment of previous lives. Reincarnation is the outcome of our previous actions. We have to take rebirth to bear the impact of earlier deeds.

The real understanding of death gives a fresh meaning to life. First, we have to search a divine purpose in it and not to be afraid about it. A person who shuns and lacks the essence of death dies several times in life; however, other person who takes death as a divine purpose and remains prepared for it, lives a life full of purpose. Life often is spent in meeting the needs of body, while focusing on inner growth is often ignored.

When death comes suddenly, people are not ready to take it with grace.

This leads us to realize what is it that one has to leave here in this world along with body consciousness, and what are the things one can hold on to inner consciousness. All wealth, possessions, self-ego, power, authority, respect along with body will go away from us. However, actions (Karma), whether good or bad creates certain impressions on inner self (soul) and these actions stays with it and forms part of belongings that moves from this life to another life.

A person who takes death as reality that can come at any time, looks at life from the perspective of temporary abode. His focus will be to bring inner calmness through purification of soul by way of love, devotion, sincerity, gratitude and compassion. Whatever he does, be it job, attend to family, focus will be to fulfil the bigger purpose, to bring peace and inner calmness. The more we think about death, better it is to realize futility of so many things that are going to be with us for a temporary period.